Phil Beadle won the Secondary Teacher of the Year Award in 2004. He writes a regular column about education in the *Guardian* and featured in the Channel 4 series *The Unteachables*. He lives in South East London with his wife and three children.

D0626217

www.rbooks.co.uk

Could Do Better!
Help Your Child Shine at School

Phil Beadle

CORGI BOOKS

TRANSWORLD PUBLISHERS
61–63 Uxbridge Road, London W5 5SA
A Random House Group Company
www.rbooks.co.uk

COULD DO BETTER!
A CORGI BOOK: 9780552155113

First published in Great Britain
in 2007 by Doubleday
a division of Transworld Publishers
Corgi edition published 2008

Addresses for Random House Group Ltd companies outside the UK
can be found at: www.randomhouse.co.uk
The Random House Group Ltd Reg. No. 954009

Penguin Random House is committed to a sustainable future for
our business, our readers and our planet. This book is made from
Forest Stewardship Council® certified paper.

Printed and bound in Great Britain by Clays Ltd, Elcograf S.p.A.
Typeset in Goudy Old Style

2 4 6 8 10 9 7 5 3 1

To my mum, Olive Bridget Beadle, whose interest in my education is the reason I am able to write a book.

Contents

Foreword

I come from a large family. Mum and Dad have five siblings each, which when you add them all together means I have a brother, a sister, twenty uncles and aunts and twenty-four cousins. There is no real history of academic achievement in our family. This is not to say they are not clever. They are. Very. But my family's history is one of working with our hands: my mum, dad, aunts and uncles all left school as soon as they were able. Dad's job involves being outside in freezing cold weather working with unforgiving pieces of metal, which occasionally bite. He has spent his days, in his own words, 'up to his neck in grease and shit'. It's a very hard way of making a living. He still does it, at the age of sixty-two.

Despite the fact that her schooling finished at an early age, Mum respected education as a path out of dangerous and physically uncomfortable work, and she taught me to read at the age of four. My first day at school involved a reading test with Mrs O'Brien. I can still recall her look of astonishment, along with my own sense of pride, as I rattled fluently through book after book of the 'Peter and Jane' series.

For someone from my family to have written for a broadsheet newspaper and to have published a book is outside the realms of what we would expect for ourselves. These achievements are entirely attributable to the interest my mother took in my education, and the continued sense she gave me that I was in some way special.

Your own involvement in the education your child receives is still the single biggest key to him leading a life which is as exciting and as rewarding as you would want it to be. You, the parent, have the power and the ability to transform your child's chances in life just as my own mum did mine.

Your child is special. It may be that you bought this book because it seems nobody sees this at the moment, least of all the child himself. But there is a tipping point. All your child needs to set out on the path towards being something truly special is to have just one person believe in him, one person to take an interest and let him know how special he is and could be. You are that one person in your child's life. Believe in your child and you will be giving him one of the most precious gifts it is in your power to give.

Introduction

On the day before he went to big school for the first time, I asked my son Len to draw me a house.

Now you'd probably expect a four-year-old to just dive in. Not Len. He licked his lips, looked me in the eyes, and held a pause in which acres spread to galaxies before asking, 'Is it a spooky house?'

I wasn't expecting such a difficult question, so I thought a bit, shrugged, and said, 'Yeah, I think it probably is.'

He couldn't quite see it, however, so he carried on questioning.

'Is it an alien house?'

'I see no reason why not,' I replied, pleased with my son's natural inquisitiveness.

But it can take more than a glib brush-off to satisfy Len. He thought for a moment, took in a huge gulp of breath, and then delivered the ultimate Len-question.

'Is it the darkness?'

I was flummoxed. Is it the darkness? What on earth does that mean? Struggling for a way to understand the question, I blurted out, 'What, the band?'

'No, not the band, silly.' Len often gets cross with the obtuseness of adults. 'Is . . . the . . . house . . . Da-AA-a-a-rk-NES-S-S-s-s?'

Metaphor is one of the highest order forms of creativity, and Len speaks it fluently, unquestioningly, without any awareness of being at all clever, at the age of four. I resolved to come up with an answer of suitable poetic complexity.

'Uh, yeah,' I managed.

He had the bit between his teeth now. 'Could it be the spookiest house in the whole of your world of men?'

'Absolutely, Len. Draw me the spookiest house in the whole of my world of men.'

Having checked he knew exactly what I wanted, he nodded to himself and set to the task, and after much chewing of the tongue, he eventually produced something with which he was quite rightly chuffed.

Now, if you ask an eight-year-old, or even an adult, to draw you a house, you'll generally get the same result: a square box, four equidistant windows, rectangular door in the middle, triangle on top, out of which rises a chimney pouring out a single, lonely wisp of curling smoke. Which, let's face it, looks nothing like any house you'd see on your street.

Len's house, however, was a whole other can of beans. It was multi-coloured for a start. The wall on the right was four times thicker than that on the left, 'Because the winds blow heavier on that side, silly.' It had three chimneys belching out colour-coded smoke, which, Len informed me, indicated their relative heats: 'Brown is for hot. Black is for very hot. Orange is super hot!' Noddy stickers were festooned on the outer walls to remind everyone it was a children's house, and there were hundreds of eyes where you would normally expect the windows to be, not only because it was an alien house, but also to put off the many robbers who ply their trade in our part of Catford.

It was a fantastically imaginative piece of work. Len, like all four-year-olds, is a stone-cold, hard-wired, dyed-in-the-wool, certifiable, no messing about, absolute complete and utter bloody genius. He routinely asks fantastic questions I can't answer.

'What's water made of?'

'Dunno.'

'What do ducks eat when there's no one feeding them bread?'

'Dunno. Dirt?'

'Why is a petrol station called a station?'

'Dunno.'

'Why don't people fall off the earth when it turns around?'

'Gravity.'

'What's gravity?'

'Dunno.'

'Would a big rocket be crushed in a black hole, and a very small one get through? If fire can harm metal, why can't metal harm fire? Why do we close our eyes when we are scared? How do we know that electricity exists if we can't see it? Where exactly is the future? Is it over here or over there?'

'It's anywhere you want it to be, Len.'

The next day, with a richly deserved sense of genuine achievement filling his small frame, he toddled off happily, a four-year-old version of Jim Morrison carrying an empty pack folder, to his first day at big school. After lunch he came back excited, brandishing another picture he'd drawn, and with which he was equally pleased: a square box with four equidistant windows, rectangle in the middle, triangle on the top and a chimney from which smoke curled skywards.

Len had entered the British education system, and the process of attrition through which the genius of children is mercilessly ground away had kicked in (with a vengeance) on the first day of his formal schooling.

Every Child Can Achieve

Human beings are social animals. We like to fit in; we don't like to stand out too much. However, much of the socialization process we inflict on children at school merely enforces conformity, regimentation and standard response and opinion. Many of the attitudes and structures still present in our education system have been hanging around since the beginning of the industrial age. Some classroom layouts feel decidedly pre-industrial. Eyes forward.

Listen to me. Backs straight. Shut up.

Your children should not be forced into any such boxes of conformity. They don't fit them. Children are not battery hens, and any form of education that treats them as mere factory products is dehumanizing and destructive.

Any push towards conformity and regimentation can strip away the unmitigated genius and purity of children's thinking, replacing it with a thin, watery gruel of inherited behaviour and thought. The quality of thinking that produces a standard, generic, that's-nothing-like-a-house picture of a house is unlikely to solve the problem of global warming. Intellects with the unfettered brilliance of a four-year-old just might.

The poet W. B. Yeats described education as 'not the filling of a pail, but the lighting of a fire', and he was right. But there is increasingly a lot of pail-filling in British education, a lot of box-ticking and pointless paperwork, which does not advance children's education in any way at all.

Several years ago, I witnessed a primary school teacher telling a group of very small children a story about a caterpillar, a moth and a light bulb. The moth's attraction to the light was fatal, she said. Far better to remain the slug-like caterpillar and stay safe than to leave the chrysalis and get ideas above their station. This woman was paid to give children the insidiously corrosive message that it is better not to try for things that might initially seem beyond you, that it is better not to have dreams, and if you can't fight them off then it is best never to try to realize them. She was an idiot. It's far better to try bravely, to fail gloriously, and then to get up, brush yourself off and go about constructing another fantastic failure than it is to stay safe and never give yourself the chance to become all the amazing things you could one day be.

If I have an educational philosophy, it is this: a belief in the innate, untutored brilliance of every child; a belief that if you have the ability to recognize and reward the genius in a child, to address it directly, you will hand her the gift of a profoundly positive attitude to learning, study and hard work.

Every child can achieve. Every single one of them. But sometimes you have to rub a little dirt off first to find the brightest jewels.

A number of years ago I taught a bottom-set Year 9 English class (thirteen- and fourteen-year-olds) who, it was felt, were the ultimate in poisoned chalices for a double period on a windy Wednesday afternoon. This class of 'write-offs' contained jewels beyond measure.

Will and Charlie were inseparable. Both wheelchair-bound, they travelled in together each morning on the same school bus. They were fantastic kids, but some people had assumed that because their legs didn't work too well, somehow this must also have affected their brains. It hadn't. Will and Charlie hadn't shown much of their talents in lessons thus far in their schooling, but that didn't mean that they weren't there. All it took, in fact, was for a copy of Shakespeare's *Romeo and Juliet* to be plonked on their desk. They devoured it. 'It's f***ing mega, this book, sir,' they'd say in unison. After telling them off for using the word 'mega', I eventually cast them as the murderers in the school production of *Macbeth*, in which they were suitably brilliant, if a bit cheeky: Charlie describing me to another teacher as looking like 'a vampire in need of a damn good night out'. (He popped in to see me some time after he had left school, accompanied by a very nice and very pretty girl. His arm muscles bulged as he told me all about how he had just completed the London Marathon in his wheelchair.)

Also in that class was Patricia, who had arrived from Spain and who was automatically put in the bottom set because she couldn't speak English (a practice the idiocy of which never ceases to amaze me). Walking along the corridors one afternoon, I noticed her sitting quietly, engrossed in a volume of the poems of Federico

García Lorca (in Spanish). I stopped, gobsmacked (Lorca is a difficult though ultimately rewarding read), and mouthed with my customary eloquence, 'Wow. Bloody 'ell, Patricia. Lorca? Fantastic.' She puffed up, clutching the book to her chest and proudly jutting out her chin. 'Sir,' she said, 'I lahv Lorca.' She might not have been able to say more than a few words in English at that point, but she was a genius in her own language. She went on to study linguistics at university. Before leaving school, she left a note on my desk that said, simply, 'Thank you. You are the one who change my life.' I still hadn't got as far as teaching her to bung a 'd' on the end of a verb when it's in the past tense.

These are just three of the children in the bottom set of a school in one of the less celebrated areas in the country. Sometimes the education system allows such magical children as these to fall through the cracks, when all it takes for them to blossom is for one person to believe in them, to praise them, to take a stand on their behalf. If the only person in your child's life who is prepared to convey total belief in her abilities is you, her parent, then that is enough.

I have never taught a child I did not like. There is something unique and special about every single one of them. They may have different levels of potential, may offer differing levels of challenge, but that doesn't mean any one is better than any other. Their potentials may all be different, but they have a right to reach that potential, whatever it is.

Some kids are so special as to require extra support. School teachers are graduate professionals, and generally if special treatment is needed this will be picked up fairly early on. However, if you feel that your child is not progressing at the rate you'd expected, and you have good reason to suspect that she has a specific learning difficulty, then you should contact her class teacher in the first instance, or the special educational needs coordinator (SENCO) if you get no joy. If your child has a serious learning difficulty, she may qualify for a statement of special educational needs, which will entitle her to in-class support. The process of obtaining this statement can be lengthy, though, and can require tenacity on the part of the parent.

I repeat, no child is beyond hope. With the input of the professionals who work with kids with special needs, fantastic transformations can take place. I've seen boys with cerebral palsy take lead roles in school plays and score A grades in speaking and listening, and I've watched a child with just such a disability go on to enjoy a successful career in the theatre.

What Is Education For?

'What is education for?' is a profound philosophical question, one that has reverberated off walls for centuries. Part of it is to instil an understanding that there is a link between the depth of your labours and the quality of your joy, that happiness is the accidental by-product of positive action. However, it is also more than this. A good teacher will nurture a questioning spirit in a child, foster her doubt and give her the equipment she needs to challenge the certainties of previous generations. A good education should teach the value of the past and the mistakes we have made. Above all, it is its own reward.

The process of learning should be exciting, enlivening and, more often than not, anarchic. It should ignite passions that will carry on into adult life. It should make children aware that each and every one of them is in possession of her own unique combination of gifts, talents and competencies. It should also teach them, in direct opposition to a lot of what goes on in schools, that conformity of thought and behaviour is not necessarily a good thing.

The teacher who had the most impact on me as a child, Mr

Latham, and to whom I owe more than he will probably ever realize, allowed me to experiment in lessons without fear of censure. When I should have written an essay, often he'd find a bad (and I mean really bad) poem on his desk. He didn't complain about this, almost tacitly encouraging it: he knew that playing about with stuff was a part of being fifteen, and let me discover for myself that if I did it in an exam I would not get the results he wanted for me.

Britain's manufacturing industry is spent. We are in an age where our chief export is intellectual property. To design fantastic new things that people will want to buy, we need a nation of people who can dream things up, not simply regurgitate and obey. The 'regurgitate and obey' jobs are either on the wane or are being monopolized by more adaptable immigrant workers. Our children need, increasingly these days, to be taught not what to think, but how to think for themselves. Of course education should aim to instil a work ethic, but not through some externally imposed, Orwellian-style 'work is good' diktat. Work doesn't always lead to freedom: the legend ARBEIT MACHT FREI above the entrance to Auschwitz is the most blackly ironic proof of this. Low-paid, repetitive hard work can be a prison inflicted on those born in one environment by those from another.

However, a cliché such as 'hard work brings its own reward' becomes a cliché only because truth is a virus: you may try to stop it spreading, but it'll find a way. There is no guarantee in life that hard work in school will lead to good exam grades, which will, in turn, lead to a rewarding and fulfilling job, and thence, inevitably, to a happy emotional life. It can fall down at any point. But if children don't engage positively with the idea of a proper day's graft, then the acquisition of what constitutes, to most, a happy life is left to luck. And luck ain't always around when you need it. Success comes through practice and determination, and through deciding to make the most of what your genes have gifted you.

Discipline and Rules

I'm not a great fan of externally imposed forms of discipline, particularly those of the punitive variety. Discipline is something you locate in yourself; it cannot be provided for you. If it is, you become reliant on other people for it.

The present government has been responsible for propounding some truly unpleasant and idiotic ideas about discipline over the last few years, in particular the repulsive policy of 'zero tolerance'. It's a direct reversal of the views of the English philosopher and social reformer Jeremy Bentham. Where he proposed that the punishment should fit the crime, so that judges aren't allowed to confuse the smoking of a joint with mass genocide, some bright spark in the American judiciary decided to dispense with this rational perspective and make every offence a hanging offence.

When applied to the world of education, it is not only a vile way to treat children, but is, of course, entirely impotent. You cannot automatically exclude every child who farts in class on the basis that doing so will stop everyone else from farting. Schools built for a thousand kids would be populated solely by one extremely pale and nervous boy shuddering by a window as he tries desperately, vainly, to hold on to a fart that is determined to sneak out. The rest of the school population would be frolicking in the park, smoking joints, committing genocide and rightly flipping the finger to the unemployed truant officer.

This is not to say that I disagree with rules, of course. Children need and like rules. When a supply teacher turns up for a lesson in a school, the kids will let out an initial whoop of joy that they will be able to sod about all lesson, but that whoop never truly convinces. In reality, they are disappointed. Children know that education is important, and that the rules are the boundaries set by adults to keep them safe. When the supply teacher turns up, what the kids are actually doing is worrying. 'Am I safe? Will I learn anything at all this lesson?' By setting rules for your own children you are showing you care about their safety. They may kick against them, but in reality they're glad that rules exist and are rigidly enforced. The fact that you set areas beyond which your children cannot go, means they can have fun in safety; the rules provide the structure within which your child can be intellectually anarchic and discover fantastic things. Rules at school exist for exactly the same reason, and your child should treat them with the absolute respect you require of her at home. That is not to say that she won't get things wrong from time to time. She will, but provided that the teacher is not one of those unimaginative bores who sees rules as religion, your child will serve only a token penance and be quickly forgiven.

Where there is conflict in school between your child and either an individual teacher or the institution itself, there is one sure way of ensuring this passes by with the minimum of fuss and damage. It can be difficult to stomach for some parents, but is sane and vital advice none the less.

Always take the side of the teacher.

The vast majority of teachers are absolutely lovely; gentle, kind and intelligent human beings. They have entered the profession because they like children, and will always attempt to do their best for them. They do not relish conflict with the children they are employed to inspire, but if your child has consistently broken a school rule, the teacher has a responsibility to all the kids in the class to do something about it. If your child has been doing something in school she shouldn't, the teacher is not doing his job properly if he lets it pass. Talented graduate professionals with years of experience do not lie just to get children into trouble. If anything, the only time they are ever likely to dispense with the truth is to keep them out of it. Many children, however, will happily tell any lie, no matter how outrageous, and will defend it to the death if they think it will get them out of a hole. This includes your children and mine. So trust the teacher. He will guide you and your child through any disciplinary problems as quickly and painlessly as possible. Where it goes wrong is when parents storm up to the school screaming, 'My Johnny never lies! He's just not capable of it!' This doesn't help anyone. The teacher will see you as a psychopath, and within half an hour the whole staff will know this – and will avoid your child. Don't do it, no matter how plausible your child's story.

In terms of rules at home as to completion of homework, and studying at home, this is really up to you. There are those who think children should get their school bag out the moment they've passed the threshold, and those who think it should wait till after dinner. The solution is to ask your child when she feels she studies best, and to let her do it this way (provided it is not in fact merely a skilful work-avoidance tactic). Any system that ensures homework is taken seriously and is not copied from a mate in the ten minutes before the start of a lesson will suffice.

Praise – the Great Motivator

The key means of motivation and class management used in the school environment is praise. If a naughty boy isn't doing what he is meant to – sitting down, for instance – teachers, rather than turn purple and scream at them, will focus on a child who is doing what's required. Not because the obedient child is a much shyer, more malleable human being, and is therefore easier to pick on. The teacher doesn't pick on the obedient child. He's nice to him. Keeping his focus entirely on the kid who's doing what's required, the teacher lavishes praise on him. 'Well done, John. Thanks for doing that so quickly. And I've noticed – and this is fantastic

– that every time you always get your stuff out at the beginning of the lesson. You never have to be asked, and you've always got the right equipment. Love those shoes by the way, and that haircut's great.' By the time the teacher has turned round, naughty boy has sat down and got out his equipment for the first time in years. He's sitting up straight. He's even combed his hair.

Everyone likes praise. Eight till eighty. It is the simplest and easiest applied of psychologies. As an employee, if someone tells me to do something or else, he'll have a long wait; give me a bit of praise, however, and I'll jump through fire for him. The same applies to children. If you want your child to do her homework, you don't need to make threats or promises of treats, just start praising the last piece she did.

The praise you dole out has to be descriptive, otherwise you'll find yourself in the position of a deputy head teacher under whom I served, who would start every assembly with a scattergun of indiscriminate praise – 'That's great!' 'That's fantastic!' 'That's brilliant!' – until one time a child had the guts to ask exactly what was so great, fantastic and brilliant? This flummoxed the deputy head so completely that he replied, 'I don't know, but it's great, isn't it?' There's simply no point in just serving up any old flannel. You'll be rumbled in double quick time. In class, I'll single out a child and go to town on specifics. 'Jenny, I think your listening skills have been fantastic all lesson. You've kept your eyes on me, your body language is inclined towards me, and it's really helped me that you've been able to do this.' If you are seeking to motivate your child to engage with her homework, then go to town on specific praise, describing exactly what was so good about what she did last time, and how you think she'd be able to do it even better this time, and you'll find she is, suddenly and miraculously, in a better frame of mind to approach the task.

Engagement

In truth, children only really mess about in lessons because they are bored. The solution is obvious: don't bore them. My way of keeping a class from chucking paper airplanes at my head is to make sure that what they are doing is more interesting than preparing and launching papyrus missiles. And if the need to chuck a paper airplane at teacher's bonce is so intense as to be irresistible, I'll give permission to do so, provided the first sentence of a story has been written on it. Another child can then pick it up from the front of the class and write down another line before folding it up again and sending it flying towards teacher's throbbing forehead.

One of the main challenges facing teachers in the twenty-first century is the attention span of the children they are teaching. When a child's attention has wandered, you can shout all you want, upbraid all you like. It's unlikely you'll get that attention back.

I've found there's a simple way to retain children's attention, and through this to inspire them: the more activities you get through when they are learning, the more different approaches you take to the same problem, the more they will retain that heightened state of alertness and near excitement they'll need to make them associate learning with pleasure. Children become bored quickly with any formulaic approach, so one of the key skills to keeping them engaged is to surprise them, continually.

When teachers ask me about my teaching style, I reply that, with the exception of crack, Campari and Catholicism, they should try everything. There is no idea too far out of left field for the brilliant minds they are teaching, no idea the children they teach can't understand. Often the best way in is that which many would instantaneously reject as being unworkable or too far out. You've got to go to the cliff edge, because that's where the prettiest flowers grow.

So, this book is packed with many different approaches to learning, all of which can be mixed and matched to suit the individual child. If you are helping your child grapple with a piece of homework, or attempting to help her in her revision for an exam, you could do worse than randomly select an activity from each of the seven chapters from 2 to 8 and complete them (again, in a random manner) over the space of fifty minutes. At the point when her attention starts to flag with one approach, switch immediately to another. If one seems to be working really well, stick with it; if one doesn't work at all, chuck it immediately without feeling guilty. The more different ways of learning your child becomes fluent in, the more she will get out of her education and the more personal reward and satisfaction you will get from helping her discover things.

Protecting Your Child from Pressure

You may have picked this book up because you are entering the parents' nightmare, which is your child's transition from primary to secondary. If this is the case, I empathize. Alternatively, you may be worried about what you see as a lack of progress, and you're looking for ideas with which to kick-start your child's efforts. You may be approaching exams and be seeking tips as to how you can ensure your child gets the best grades she possibly can. The exercises in the book are applicable for all ages, and if you use any of them at regular intervals I guarantee they'll boost your child's levels of attainment and her enjoyment of, and success in, learning.

A big warning, though. Under no circumstances is this book to be used to whack kids around the head, telling them they're lazy. Its function is to ignite a joy in learning, not to add to the pressures they are already under. You received more homework than your parents, and the amount of homework your own children may come home with may well frighten you. It's a competitive world, and since Mr Blair identified his three main priorities as education, education, education, the school system in Britain and the humans working in it – children and teachers – have been forced to endure unbelievable pressure.

League tables may have given parents a (sometimes inaccurate) indication of whether a school is good or not, but they are blunt instruments which have been used to inflict a murderous bludgeoning on innocents. Any system that measures the achievements of a top private school, where they train an economic and social elite to pass exams, as being of more value than those of schools where refugee children's wounds are tended, non-English speakers become fluent, and children from families with generations of antipathy towards the idea of education reverse those years of conditioning and achieve, is clearly idiotic by design. But league tables are not going away any time soon, and all the time they are there, the head teacher at your local school will be judged not on the quality of the environment she provides for your child, or on the fact that your child is happy, but on the number of children she gets to jump over a bar, the height of which has been fairly arbitrarily set. If she does not get an acceptable number of children over this bar, she won't keep her job very long. So she'll pass this pressure for exam results on to her staff, who will pass it, in turn, on to the children they teach. As a result, your child will come home from school stressed out with mountains of homework she doesn't understand and unmanageable demands on her organizational abilities. The much-trumpeted improvements in British education are real, but they are a sandcastle built on the early graves of teachers and the crushed spirits and underused imaginations of children. Ten per cent of the children in our schools, and probably a vastly higher proportion of our teachers, are clinically depressed. This startling statistic is a direct result of a politician taking the easy populist line that the standards in our schools are not good enough.

If your child's school is placing her under too much pressure, denying her the right to a happy, carefree childhood, the only person liable to protect her is you. If your child has too much homework, let the school know that you think the demands they make are unreasonable. I heard a story about a history teacher in the 1980s who set a first-year secondary-school pupil the task of copying out the whole of the Old Testament as a punishment by nine o'clock the following morning. The poor child's mother rang the teacher late that evening, sobbing. He had managed to get only halfway through the Book of Genesis; could he have an extension? In the old days, a teacher would do something like this as a fairly unconscionable joke. Nowadays, it would be seen as an entirely reasonable demand.

The Joy of Education

Children's happiness and self-esteem are vastly more important than the set of grades they receive from an exam board. Your child is far more likely to live a happy and productive life if her right to a positive view of herself is upheld staunchly. It is this positive self-image that is the surest indicator of academic success, so it is vital for your child's education and her life that you, her parent – who is, after all, the key determining factor to her thinking positively about herself – understand that this is the most important of all parenting skills.

Education can denude childhood of its magic, replacing joy with grind. Parents and teachers must understand that the brilliance and enthusiasm with which my son Len approached his drawing of a house need to be maintained throughout a child's school career. In Denmark, not only do they not bother teaching kids to read until they are about eight, but when a child's attention seems to be flagging they dispense with the books, take the child outside and twirl them around. Before they are eight, they concentrate on play and on talking. Reading is a pleasure. If children associate it with early struggle and failure rather than with play, they will not want to do it. Denmark has what is described as a 'far higher literacy outcome' than Britain, which, as even the government admits, speaks for itself.

A positive self-image combined with a nurtured joy in learning will inevitably lead to good results. Studies carried out in top girls' schools have found that the pressure to attain a string of A* grades is so intense, so all-consuming, that the girl who attains only As and Bs regards herself as a failure; moreover, this gnawingly corrosive self-image stays with her for ever, affecting her work and relationships. This will not happen if you teach your child that learning is of value for its own sake, and the grades, if they come (which they will), are incidental.

The point of this book is to give you, the parent, an insight into your child and her capabilities, and into some of the stuff that goes on day after day in the classroom; to let you know of the developments in teaching in the last ten years; and to give you access to them so that you may use them with your own children, and infuse them with the sense that learning is fantastic fun. As a friend of mine, one Jason Miller, said recently, 'Work's got to be fun, hasn't it? Otherwise it's just that . . . work.'

There are two key messages I'd like you to take with you, which serve as the bedrock on which any dealings I have with children are based.

The first of these is stolen from the educationalist David Keeling, who in *The Big Book of Independent Thinking* flags up the fact that each child has two voices in her head. One, to use David's exact words, tells her, 'You're crap, you're useless, don't bother, they'll only laugh at you when you get it wrong'; the other voice says, 'You're beautiful, you're talented, you're fantastically bright, and you've got that extra little bit of flair they haven't got. Go get 'em, tiger! Knock 'em dead!' If you, as a parent, can make sure your child goes to school knowing that the first voice is an impostor, you'll have given her every chance to succeed.

The final and most important message is one I inherited from my first and best teachers, my own mum and dad. I received two pieces of guidance at the time of my O levels from my family. The first, from my maternal grandfather – if I was stressed out before an exam and wanted a couple of Valium, he'd be more than happy to bung me a few – was probably not the best piece of help ever handed out. The second message, from Mum and Dad, was profoundly more useful: 'Your best is good enough.' If your child can come home from school, from an exam, a game of hockey or a drama competition, and say honestly to the mirror that she did her best, then you have no right whatsoever to ask anything more of her. It doesn't matter whether she wins or not. If she is able to look at herself after the event and know that she gave her best, then she will always, in whatever circumstance life presents, be good enough.

Repeat this to your children regularly and it will nourish them on the path of their lives.

Your Child's Unique Genius:

Multiple Intelligences and Learning Styles

Kelsey Park School for Boys wasn't called that for nothing. It was opposite Kelsey Park, and there weren't any girls there.

We were twelve, and Miss Dunderdale, our English teacher, was well thought of by the older boys. In every school in the country teachers are allocated a code that abbreviates their name, as a time-saver for busy admin staff. Mine is generally PB, or PBE. Miss Dunderdale's code was DD. She told a semi-amusing tale about how DD could stand for Double Diamond, the beer, which in the advertising slogan of the time 'worked wonders'. She claimed she was able to perform much the same function herself.

And she did work wonders. At parents' evening she showed my mum a piece of fiction I had written about catching a small shark in Cornwall and throwing it back in revulsion. She told Mum I had 'vision'. I still don't really know what this meant, but I remember her comments thirty years on.

She also did something quite stunning for a boy I knew . . .

At junior school I played football during lunch and break with a group of friends. We were a happy bunch, with no real sense of, nor care about, one another's differences, be they skin colour, relative prosperity or academic ability. On our first day at senior school we were split up into different classes. (Later, I learned that this savage rendering had a name: 'streaming'.) I sat waiting in the school hall as all my friends went off, in clumps, to other classes, till I was left with a group of twenty-nine other boys, all of whom wore glasses and spoke 'posh'. We were told we were 'academic'. Apparently, I was the only one from my old school who was 'academic', and I went off to sit with my new colleagues in quiet, studious rows in what they called 'the top set'.

Eventually, my friends from primary school and I forgot about one another – beautiful and innocent childhood friendships dissolved into nothingness. In the top set we discovered academic snobbery and an overestimated sense of our own worth. My former friends in what they then called the 'remedial class' discovered sodding about, delivering lip and bunking off. By the middle of the second year (now called Year 8) we were different species. One close friend from primary school, Alan, would not talk to me any more. I heard him referring to me as 'Beadle' in the dinner queue. He had used my first name many times in his young life, but now no longer regarded me as human enough to deserve one. I was one of the speccy kids, he was one of the lazy ones. I was saddened by this. Our parents were friends, I had been to his house. Even at the age of twelve I missed him.

One day in Miss Dunderdale's English class, Alan's name came up. One of the top-set boys said out loud, 'Oh Alan, he's thick.' I was upset by this, because, though he no longer wanted to know me, I still felt loyalty towards him. Miss Dunderdale, however, was more than upset: she was incandescent, and let rip. 'Thick?' she railed. 'Thick? Alan can take a whole car engine apart and put it back together in an afternoon. All from memory. Can you do that? Can you? Don't you ever, ever, let me hear you call another child thick again.'

She was pretty cool, Miss Dunderdale, and I think the poor top-set lad learned his lesson. I learned something really important too, and it continues to affect my work as a teacher. There's no such thing as thick. There may be children who don't know what they're good at yet, but thick doesn't exist.

Some of the more challenging children I have come across have, for some strange reason or other, got it into their heads that they are neither capable nor clever. This infection of the self-esteem is a barrier to learning, stopping them getting what they need from education. Because they struggle with certain subjects they start believing they can't do them. They can, of course. But you can't peel a potato with a hammer, and a can of beans remains shut without a tin opener. You must employ just the right mechanism to reach into a child's psyche and let him know for certain that he can achieve. He is clever, in his own completely unique way; in a different way to any human being who ever stood on planet earth before him.

MULTIPLE INTELLIGENCES

For thousands of educational practitioners across the globe, the mechanism that reaches directly into the minds of children and lets them know how special they are was conceived by an American psychologist called Howard Gardner. Gardner is one of the world's foremost authorities on human intelligence. In 1983 he came up with the Theory of Multiple Intelligences, which I believe provides just the right tin opener for reaching into children's psyches and putting back the shine their engagement with the education system may have rubbed off.

Gardner's impact on the world of education cannot be overstated. The Commissioner for London Schools, Tim Brighouse, recently went so far as to compare his theories in terms of their significance to those of Galileo, who discovered that the earth circled the sun. Brighouse is an intelligent and knowledgeable man, and I don't think he would use such hyperbole without fair reason.

Put simply, Gardner's theory is this: there is no one correct definition of intelligence. The notion of IQ is worse than useless, since it only really measures one very specific skill: the ability to crack codes. (The test for 'intelligence quotient', an objective measure of intelligence, has been writing people off as 'mental defectives' for nearly a century.) For Gardner, intelligence is actually a set of separate abilities we all have in different measure. No one intelligence is of more worth than any other, as they have all developed through evolution to keep us alive. Imagine, for instance, two cavemen confronted by a grumpy sabre-toothed tiger. While Ug, with his mathematical and logical intelligence, might be able to calculate the angle from which the tiger is approaching to the nearest degree, it is Thug, his mate with the bodily or kinetic intelligence, who in the meantime has actually run away. 'Who's the clever one now, nerdy boy?'

The point Miss Dunderdale was trying to get over was similar: my old friend Alan had a different set of intelligences to Top-set Boy. Top-set Boy could write a competent essay, sure, but Alan could do something useful. He was good with his hands. Don't underestimate being good with your hands. My dad can rewire a boiler, plaster a room, construct a kitchen and design a machine of baffling complexity on a piece of paper, and then build the bloody thing, all the while keeping a broom up his bum with which to sweep the floor. He is, in short, one of the most intelligent human beings I have ever met. But his schooling taught him otherwise.

Gardner proposes that there are seven intelligences:

Bodily/kinetic intelligence: physical intelligence, coordination, dexterity. The bodily intelligent child might be brilliant at catching, throwing or kicking a ball. They make great dancers, athletes, engineers or carpenters.

This is probably the most fascinating educationally, in that so many of our children, particularly boys, have this in high quotients, and quite often this fact is completely and conveniently ignored. It's a missed opportunity. If any teacher wants to truly engage a class, he gets them off their chairs and asks them to use their bodies in moving or making things.

It is often the case that children who struggle the most academically possess the highest quotient of bodily intelligence. A bloke being interviewed on TV while sitting opposite the presenter might clam up; but you interview him while he is fixing his car, or doing something else with his hands, and immediately he becomes articulate again. This can apply to many boys in the school system.

Inter-personal intelligence: means people skills, having the intuitive ability to show empathy towards others, and being able to communicate fluently.

A child with inter-personal intelligence is the life and soul, can relate to anyone, and doesn't appear to fear social situations. If you haven't got inter-personal intelligence, you may spend much of your school life at the side of the playground watching on enviously while everyone else plays, smiles and laughs. This intelligence is vital for going to work and school. Both environments can be pretty bleak without it.

Intra-personal intelligence: the child who has a strong internal dialogue, who possesses self-awareness, and an ability to think.

This is often, though not exclusively, found in those who have little of the inter-personal variety. Since having none of the former ensures you become a bit of a Billy No Mates, you get a lot of time on your own to think about how unfair the world is, and whether now would be the right time to invest in a black roll-neck, and start smoking Gauloises and pretending to read French writers whose names you can't pronounce.

Those with strong intra-personal intelligence are worth going the extra mile for. They may not necessarily be gregarious, may not even say much, but the fact they have thought deeply about the world and their place in it means that when they do say something, it will usually be worth listening to.

Visual/spatial intelligence: awareness of space and of shapes; a strong sense of the visual – for example, the ability to navigate unfamiliar streets, or to make sense of the world through its visual representation.

I don't have any of this type of intelligence. My wife sometimes makes me wander around art galleries. I go, grudgingly. While she launches into paroxysms of wonder about a pile of bricks that is pretending to be something else, I look on dumbly, convinced that the entire artistic worth of the works contained in the Tate Modern is of less value than a mandolin line on an Eagles B-side; and that the Turbine Hall in the aforementioned gallery looks like a bloody good place to keep a turbine.

People who have a high quotient of visual intelligence think in pictures. Incidents from their life leave fat, great, dirty footprints on their cerebral cortex. The plethora of television programmes featuring people designing things, or making over houses, are made to appeal to people with strong visual intelligence. If, when people on such programmes start talking in tones of awed wonder about 'clean functional lines' and 'space', you haven't got a clue what they are going on about, it is because, like me, you have little visual intelligence. (Alternatively, it might be because whatever 'space' there is is being filled with aural effluent.)

Musical intelligence: the ability to memorize a musical phrase, hold a tune, or execute a spoken or musical phrase with sensitivity and grace.

There are those of us who couldn't hit a note if it were a cow's arse with a banjo. Then there are those who can pick up any musical instrument and play it almost instantaneously. An ability with or a love of music is a joyful thing that enriches the lives of those who possess it. It should have a more prominent place in British classrooms than it has currently. I once read that the subject of English is 'a mercury amongst baser metals' in that it infiltrates every other area of the school curriculum. Music does not. It should.

Logical/mathematical intelligence: the ability to work things out, to take a step-by-step approach to a complex problem – for instance, the deductive reasoning needed to play chess well.

As a little gift to unreconstructed chauvinists, this is one of the intelligences that shows up more often in the profile of men: the ability to apply logic and reason, to break a large task into small pieces, and in doing so not be put off by the size of a job. People with a high degree of this type of intelligence can work through the details of a problem step by step, and deduce an answer; but they are often less good at dealing with the emotional side of things.

Linguistic/verbal intelligence: a talent for words; the ability to read, write and speak well.

If your children are masters of language, love reading books and are difficult to shut up once they've got going, they are likely to have a heavyweight linguistic intelligence, and you should avoid arguments with them.

As I said, multiple intelligences are a way into any child's psyche, and in the following chapters I will revisit each one of these intelligences. Using them, we can redefine children's sense of themselves, particularly those who have had the millstone of failure hung around their necks, and who have been turned into hunchbacks as a result. People live up (or down) to our expectations of them. Call a child an idiot often enough and you'll have an idiot. Rephrase your sense of them so that they are aware of and proud of their specific abilities, however trivial these may seem, and the butterfly will soon emerge from its chrysalis.

Multiple intelligences test

If, before you read on, you want to get an idea of what your child's predominant intelligences are, and where his particular skills and interests lie, you could do worse than go through the following questionnaire with him. Do it in the same light-hearted spirit with which you'd do one of those lifestyle quizzes in a tabloid on a Sunday, the kind that asks questions like 'Are you good in bed?', 'How good a mother are you?', or 'Are you a crap parent, and should you feel really, really, really guilty about it?'

If your child scores lower in some areas than in others, this doesn't mean he has little intelligence in this area; and it doesn't mean that you should only read the chapters of the book in whose subject matter he scored highest. The idea is solely that you work out where his strengths lie, and therefore the forms of tuition from which he would most benefit. If, for example, it turns out that your child has high quotients of musical and linguistic intelligence, you would do well to guide him in the direction of learning things through songs and words. If he has high quotients of inter-personal and visual intelligence, it makes sense to use pictures and debate as key means of learning.

Bodily/kinetic

Do you take part in competitive sport?
Do you find it difficult to sit still for long periods of time?
Are you male?
Do you have your best ideas when you are walking?
Have you ever been in a fight?
Do you enjoy rough and tumble games with your parents?
Do you like to be cuddled?

Inter-personal

Can you count and name ten or more close friends?

Do you class yourself as an extrovert?

Do you enjoy parties?

When working in groups, do you act as the group leader, or as the one who gets others involved?

Would you say, generally speaking, that you like people?

Do you find social situations easy?

On your first day at school, did you feel reasonably confident?

Intra-personal

Would you class yourself (or have others ever classified you) as a deep thinker?

Do you prefer to be on your own?

Are you shy?

Do you have an interest in philosophy/psychology?

Do you prefer to take a while to mull over things before you make a decision?

Do you keep a diary and hide it?

Do you have only a very few close friends?

Visual/spatial

Would you ever visit an art gallery out of choice?

Do you recall your dreams easily?

Can you think of an image you would never want to see again?

Do you have posters or paintings on display in your home?

Have you changed the layout of your room, or painted any part of it this year?

Do you have your hair cut more than three times a year?

Have you bought yourself new clothes this month?

Musical

Do you have a significant collection of CDs (over ten is significant for a child)?

When you are working, do you prefer to have music on?

Do you own a musical instrument? (It doesn't matter if you can't play it.)

Can you identify more than five different genres of music?

When listening to music, do you ever think of ways in which it could be improved?

Do you ever find yourself miming a musical instrument?

Do you find the tunes to songs easy to remember?

Logical/mathematical

Do you enjoy solving problems involving numbers?

Have you ever done a sudoku puzzle?

Can you accurately estimate the height or weight of something just by looking at it?

Do you have a good sense of direction?

Do you class yourself as being good at maths?

When you have a big piece of work to do, are you able to break it down into smaller parts to make it seem easier?

Do you have a fairly good head for money?

Linguistic/verbal

Do you enjoy crosswords?

Do you keep a diary?

Have you read more than two works of fiction this year?

Do you find the words to songs easy to remember?

Would you class yourself (or would others class you) as articulate?

Do you enjoy writing stories, and are they well received?
Do you enjoy consulting a dictionary?

Now tot up the number of times your child answered 'yes' for each intelligence. You should have a score out of seven for each area. The top two, three or (in the case of a score draw) even four scores will indicate what your child's predominant strengths are. They may also provide the techniques with which he'll find it easiest to learn.

LEARNING STYLES

This is the other educational theory dominating British classrooms in the early twenty-first century. It is a separate theory to multiple intelligences, though there's some crossover, and a decent teacher might use both ideas in tandem as the bedrock on which to construct fantastic lessons.

You have five senses – taste, smell, touch, sight and hearing – and it is through these, and these alone, that you take in new information. Spiderman, of course, has 'spidey sense', but this applies only in the cases of a select few children, usually those with the mild autistic disorder Asperger's syndrome. Now, there's not a vast amount that can be done in a mainstream classroom with either 'spidey sense', taste or smell. You rarely see lessons devoted to smell or taste alone. I once saw a science teacher illustrate the concept of diffusion by spraying perfume over the heads of her students, and there are English teachers who give their students sweets and ask them to write about the taste. This is all good stuff, but you'll never hear teachers referring to students as being either olfactory or gustatory learners. There are good reasons for this. Imagine, for instance, a parent approaching his child's form tutor with, 'I'm sorry, my Johnny can't do comprehension. He is a gustatory learner. He has to take in all new information through his sense of taste.' The poor teacher trying to write an individual learning plan for Johnny would have several challenges to meet: 'twenty-nine members of the class will read a book, Johnny will eat the book'; 'twenty-nine members of the class will mix sulphuric and nitric acid, Johnny will drink it'; 'twenty-nine members of the class will play football in the dirt . . .' I could go on.

I would also have worries about being in a locked classroom with a child who is expressive in the olfactory area.

In the real world, teachers refer to what are called 'the three main learning styles': visual (sight), auditory (hearing) and kinetic (feeling), or VAK. The idea is that we take in most new information through either seeing it, hearing it or touching it. Some propose that each of us has a preferred way of taking in new information and that, as with the intelligences, we have our own profile of preferred learning styles. For instance, your child might be 50 per cent visual, 30 per cent auditory and 20 per cent kinetic. This would mean that he learns best through looking at pictures, maps and diagrams, or other visual stimuli.

I've seen stuff in lessons that would seem to bear out this theory. Many boys seem to have a preference for what is termed 'kinetic learning'. Rashid, for instance, who, unprompted, translated Macbeth's dagger speech into Lingala (a Bantu language common in central Africa) at home just because he fancied it. He performed the speech in front of the class, and eventually on a video made by the Department of Education that was sent to every school in the country. Early on in our time together Rashid could barely read when sitting down. Stand him up, though, get him moving around, and suddenly the words revealed their meaning to him, and he'd become fluent with the most difficult of texts. I've seen the effect of this kind of thing hundreds of times: kids sitting sullenly at the back of the room, failing to do any work at all lesson after lesson, suddenly becoming animated and engaged if you just ask them to move around a bit.

If you are worried that your own child is not achieving as well as he might, it could be because he is not using his preferred learning style. I have torn my hair out trying to get kids to engage in lessons that involved a lot of talking, only to find that the moment some visual stimulus was introduced they came alive. Roman, for example, who is now a graphic designer. He couldn't spell his way out of a wet paper bag, and would remain mute in speaking and listening lessons; but show him a picture or an advert and he'd be able to spot subtexts in it that would be beyond a Harvard professor.

The problem with learning styles can be assessing them correctly, as there are hundreds of different tests and they can throw up different answers. One test might tell you that your child is a kinetic learner, the other might rubbish this and tell you that he is predominantly auditory. As such, the information from the tests about preferred learning styles is pretty difficult to rely on, especially as if you take the same test on a different day it's likely you'll get a different result.

What we can say with a reasonable degree of certainty is that a teacher who teaches to only one learning style is not providing an education under which all her pupils will flourish equally. Teachers refer to lessons as having been 'VAK'd', which means that all main learning styles – visual, auditory and kinetic – were covered. A teacher who teaches a third of a lesson with visual examples, another third appealing to learners who like listening best, and the remaining third of the lesson encouraging pupils to use movement and their sense of touch, is a teacher who has given all the kids in the class at least a third of a lesson from which they can benefit.

This stuff is all a bit off-puttingly technical, I know. It is useful, though, to have some idea of the theoretical basis behind all the material in this book, which you can use to unlock the unique potential of your own child. We will occasionally have to dwell again on the more technical side of things in order to enrich your understanding of your child's education, but action is more important than theory – any idiot can have twenty good ideas before breakfast – so the rest of this book is also full of exercises you can do with your children. Hopefully, they will restore their enthusiasm in the process of education, or at the very least enrich their experience of it.

Now, let's get on with stuff you can actually do.

The Mover:
Using Your Body to Learn

He is hands on, a natural at sport or dance; loves adventure and competition; and prefers to find out things by diving straight in and doing them, rather than being told how to do them. He might also have a worrying predilection for taking things apart just to see how they work. Often the bodily intelligent child can find it very, very hard to sit still.

The notion of bodily intelligence enrages traditionalists, and I can see why some people would term it political correctness gone mad ('It's a straitjacket and a bloody good whack on the head they need, not being told they have a "different" intelligence!'). However, if the kids in class who can't sit still, who do that irritating, nervous leg-jiggling, who drum their fingers incessantly on their desks, are also the ones who have the highest bodily intelligence when assessed, surely this tells us that the version of education they're receiving is not right for them. They need something else.

Ask yourself a question. How many times in your adult life have you been forced, against your will or natural inclination, to sit stock still all day while someone you don't really respect has talked at you about a subject in which you have no interest? Furthermore, you are sat at a table with all your best mates and expressly told you must never speak to them. This form of instruction can make school a circle of hell specially designed for children.

A vast proportion of our children who struggle to sit behind desks all day cannot engage properly with the curriculum and, because of this, create discipline problems (for themselves – remember, it is the children who receive the detentions, suspensions and exclusions). There is, I think, a solid argument for a form of education that gives these kids a better chance.

In the days when eleven-year-old children were divided into successes and failures and branded as such for life (it was called the grammar school system), the inventor of the clockwork radio, Trevor Bayliss, failed his eleven plus. Mr Bayliss believes that it was wrong of the system to label him a failure. As he says of himself, 'I could barely write my own name, but I could do amazing things with meccano.' The notion of bodily intelligence respects all those young inventors, sportsmen and engineers who, like Trevor Bayliss, might be geniuses in their own field, but who leave the school system thinking they're thick.

Those like Stewart, a former pupil of mine. Stewart was over six feet tall at the age of twelve, a distractingly big hit with the girls, and completely dyslexic. Had he not attended such a great school, his inability to read and write would have left him feeling a complete failure, and that would have crossed over into his behaviour. In many schools Stewart would not have lasted the course, but in Newham we play to kids' strengths. Stewart was a superbly cultured centre-back in the Alan Hansen mould, and was encouraged to develop an interest in the scientific side of football. This grew into a love of science itself. Despite being unable to read and write at all well, Stewart left school with two A–C passes, an A grade in PE and a C in Science. He now works as a coach, earning his money developing the talents of East End kids who, like him, just need someone to believe in them and to play to their strengths. If he had not been allowed to develop his love of bodily activity, this would not have happened. He would, more likely than not, have followed a path that leads nowhere you'd want to go.

Kinetic learning is revolutionary. Some, me included, argue

that it works better than any other style of teaching. Kids love it. It is a superb way of making learning fun, addresses one of the multiple intelligences bang on the nose, and is also one of the three main learning styles. It is under-investigated, under-used and, in my opinion, the most exciting thing to happen to education since Plato was in gym socks.

There is a gender aspect to kinetic intelligence, which cannot be ignored. It is of particular use with boys, and can be the key that unlocks the door to learning for those who most suffer at the hands of the education system. To illustrate why they struggle so badly with sedentary forms of tuition, we're going to have to go all the way back to the Palaeolithic period.

A very long time ago there lived a man and a woman who spent their days huddled together for warmth in a cold, mucky cave. They had unattractively high foreheads and slack lower lips, but loved each other well enough. As an expression of this love they had babies, who demanded food, warmth and succour. Three jobs, then, between two people. Now the male troglodyte didn't much like the drudgery of keeping the fire going and changing bearskin nappies (terrible design – hard to wash), so he came up with an idea. 'Look,' he said to his unlovely companion, 'killing a mammoth is difficult. How about I do all the outside work and you just stay at home and cuddle the babies?'

She grew to regret her agreement to this, for the male had given her two jobs – providing warmth and succour – and had farmed out half of the third: for once he had brought the mammoth home, it was she who had to cook it. Every morning he'd toddle off, jawbone under one arm, leaving the cavewoman with a long list of jobs, all of which she had to accomplish with one arm as she had been left, metaphorically and literally, holding the baby.

Male and female roles polarized from that point on. Men became hunter-gatherers, and developed strong bodies, fast reflexes, a cavalier attitude to danger and a yearning for the great outdoors. Women became better at keeping a thousand different plates spinning at the same time.

Males are, by instinct and evolution, active. They are less tolerant of boredom, less able to sit still, worse at listening, and poorer at verbalizing in anything more sophisticated than grunts. All men, to a greater or lesser degree, possess a quotient of bodily intelligence that remains sadly under-recognized and under-nurtured in our school system.

While Janet can sit relatively happily and listen to a teacher drone on about left ventricles or the co-efficient of latent bananas, Johnny, generally speaking, can't. Boys don't want to *hear* about something, they want to *experience* or *do* it. If you force a boy to sit still and listen to you for more than a brief period he will more often than not start getting jiggy with it. He might start to drum his fingers on the desk. He might even forget the demands of the situation and just get up and walk over to his mate. It isn't that he is bad, or that he disrespects the teacher; it is just that he cannot cope, instinctively, with the prison in which the classroom has him placed. He is straining to *do* something.

So, what do you do with a child who won't sit still in class, who can't stop his hands from drumming on the desk, who continually scribbles and doodles when he is meant to be looking up at teacher with a benign, attentive smile and eyes full of wonder, whose body keeps making him do things that get him into trouble? You turn what is perceived as a flaw into an asset. Give the child permission to move around; allow him to get involved physically in his work; let him get his hands dirty. If a boy is getting too jiggy for the lesson, then the lesson isn't jiggy enough for the boy. And if the devil is making work for idle hands, give them something to do.

I am not a neuro-scientist. What I know about the potential of the human brain comes from practical experience with children. I have never once seen inside any of their brains, nor have I ever been tempted to dissect any of them (honestly), but there is plenty of evidence for the benefits of 'bodily' learning. Movement increases blood flow, for a start, which improves the delivery of oxygen, water and glucose to the brain, and which in turn promotes the creation of more neural networks, or connections from one part of the brain to another. The psychologist Jean Piaget even went so far as to suggest that all thought is merely suppressed movement.

Students *need* to be physically active in class. They retain knowledge longer if they connect physically and emotionally with the material they are being taught. Bodily learning works. Sometimes, when nothing else is capable of getting anywhere near reaching a child, a kinetic activity will crack this toughest of nuts and awaken in him a joy and passion for learning.

I recently did a presentation for, among others, a group of Roman Catholic monks (in mufti) at Buckfast Abbey in Devon. Though raised a Catholic, I hadn't been to church for over thirty years, but seeing as I had the family with me and there wasn't much else to do in the town of Buckfastleigh, we paid a visit to the abbey itself. On entering, I spotted a receptacle of holy water. Just to check it wouldn't burn me, I dunked my right hand in, then automatically brought it up first to my forehead, then to a point ten centimetres up from the belly button, to the left shoulder and then to the right, silently intoning as I did it, 'In the Name of the Father, and of the Son, and of the Holy Ghost.' If you had asked me outright if I knew how to do this, I probably wouldn't have been able to say (at least not without thinking about it), but my body instantly remembered, from childhood, exactly how to do it. Your body soaks up and stores away knowledge your mind is not aware it even has.

Another vital aspect of kinetic learning is that it acknowledges the importance of making, building and doing. Many of the children we teach will eventually go on to work with their hands, and an education system that thinks one form of productive activity – sitting still and writing – is of more worth than making something is an education system that knows little about the history of human achievement, and one which hates half its kids and theirs and the country's future. What is more, an education system that points at the manual jobs the fathers of many of the children do, laughing at them and calling them worthless, is not only wrong, but is classist by design. If you want to upset a working-class boy, call his dad an idiot. This is what our education system does. The almost constant suggestion that middle-class, white-collar activities are of more worth than manual work alienates and makes bitter a major part of the male school population. The attempt to superimpose middle-class values on working-class kids is, as my dad would say, a wrong 'un. Kinetic approaches to learning at least acknowledge that working with your hands and your body is valid.

Obviously, in some subjects it is much easier to dream up kinetic strategies than in others. In geography, for instance, it is pretty easy to see how making a papier mâché model of a volcano could contribute to a child's understanding; but what do you do in subjects that aren't quite as obviously tactile? How can bodily learning contribute to a child's understanding of maths, or English? Don't worry, there are solutions. One of the many beauties of bodily learning is that it is so multi-faceted. It's not just about making stuff, it's about moving, it's about gesture – it's about anything, anything at all, that engages the body.

USING ACTIONS AND GESTURES

Punctuation kung fu

Punctuation kung fu may be the archetypal method of using movement to cement learning. It featured in the Channel 4 television programme *The Unteachables*. If you didn't see it, this is what happened. A bloke in a green crombie (me) took a group of perfectly nice young people out to a farm in Suffolk. Accompanying them and spying on what they got up to was a television crew. One of the activities that seemed to chime with viewers was Crombie Man standing on a tree stump on the top of a hill going through punctuation kung fu moves with the kids (though everybody I spoke to about it, including my dad, thought I came across as a complete loony).

Punctuation kung fu works like this: all the punctuation marks are given corresponding kung fu style actions, which are accompanied by possibly racist noises imitating that great kung fu master David Carradine.

Full stop: throw a short, right-handed punch at the air in front of you. Make the noise, *Ha!*

Comma: with your right arm bent so that your hand is in front of your face, make a short twisting motion at the wrist to signify the comma shape. Make the noise, *Shi!*

Semi-colon: do the full-stop punch, then the comma shape directly underneath it. Make the noises, *Ha! Shi!*

Colon: follow the full-stop punch immediately with one directly beneath it. Make the noises, *Ha! Ha!*

Question mark: separate the curly bit into three cutting movements with the hand: one horizontal left to right, one curved around, and one vertical coming from the bottom of the curved one. Then at the bottom of the shape you have just drawn in the air, bung in a full-stop punch. Make the noises, *Shi! Shi! Shi! Ha!*

Exclamation mark: a long vertical slash, from top to bottom, followed by a full stop. Make the noises, *Shiiiiii! Ha!*

Speech marks: stand on one leg in a pose nicked from *The Karate Kid*, extend your arms diagonally to the skies and wiggle your index and middle fingers in an approximation of speech marks. Make the noise, *Haeeeee!*

Apostrophe: right arm fully extended to the air, and wiggle your index finger. Make the noise, *Blubalubaluba!* (This is the best I can do to approximate the sound you can make with your tongue when you flap it up and down against the inside of your lips.)

Ellipsis: three punches along a horizontal line. Make the noises, *Ha! Ha! Ha!*

Brackets: using your left hand first, draw a curved convex line in the air; use your right hand to do the opposite motion for the closing bracket. Make the noises, *Shi! Shi!*

Punctuation is not taught well in schools. In some cases it's not taught at all, each teacher assuming that the teacher before them will have covered something so fundamental, until you get to the stage where the child leaves school at the age of sixteen without even the vaguest conception of where a comma goes. It can be a dry old subject for kids to get their heads around, but decent punctuation is vital if a piece of writing is to communicate with any degree of sophistication. Many children, even up to GCSE level, struggle to grasp the most basic punctuation marks, so kung fu'ing them can be a really effective way to communicate each mark's function. You cannot gain a Level 4 in English at the end of Key Stage 2 without the ability to use a comma (see chapter 10), and it is attainment of this level that gives children proper access to the rest of the curriculum. Best, then, that work on punctuation is embedded early in a child's education, and that, as is the case with punctuation kung fu, it is approached in a manner likely to be memorable. And, since it is also a kinetic activity, children will be working on it with their brains and bodies properly oxygenated and therefore engaged.

Try this at home

There are two ways to use punctuation kung fu: one predominantly for fun, the other of more obvious worth.

Fun things first. A proper bout of punctuation kung fu requires three players: two combatants and a referee (I've found that it helps the referee to get into the role if he or she wears a tie round the head, perhaps even tacking on a classic Fu Manchu moustache, and maintains an inscrutable expression). The combatants face each other. The referee says the words 'capital letter', and the opponents bow to each other while repeating the same phrase. The referee then calls out three punctuation marks and the players have to put the moves and sounds for these together, in sequence, as quickly as they can. The winner is the one who puts together all three moves and their accompanying sounds correctly in the quickest time. This doesn't actually teach where the punctuation marks go, but it is devilishly difficult, hellishly funny, and is a great starter to get both brain and body working before an activity that might be more sedentary.

You can then use this knowledge to advance their learning. Photocopy a piece of text and white out all punctuation marks. Read through the piece together, and at the appointed places in the text get your child to do the kung fu punctuation move he thinks is appropriate. Alternatively, you could dictate a piece of prose, and rather than read out the punctuation, do the kung fu actions.

How's your Japanese?

Many teachers will have a story to tell about committing to memory the first ten numbers in Japanese through bodily learning, as some overpaid and underworked trainer, imported specially for the day to teach the teachers, lined us all up and asked us to scratch our knees. This is the standard introduction teachers are given to bodily learning. By learning actions to go with the first ten Japanese numbers, the teachers come to see how effective the use of gesture can be as a learning technique. The reason they asked us initially to scratch our knees was that the first two numbers in the Japanese language are 'ichi' and 'ni'. To learn these words through the kinetic method, you say 'ichi' and 'ni' while scratching your knees. Simple.

Try this at home

Each of the following numbers has a corresponding action, derived from the English word that sounds most like the Japanese number when it is spoken.

English number	Japanese equivalent	Which sounds like	As in	Accompanying movement
One	Ichi	Itchy	How you would feel if you had scabies	Start scratching . . .
Two	Ni	Knee	Where you have ligaments	. . . your knees
Three	San	Sun	The bright thing in the sky you shouldn't look at	Point to the sky

Four	Shi	She	A female	Point to a lady, if there's one handy. If not, a picture of one will do.
Five	Go go	Go go	Either a sixties nightclub at which ladies danced in bikinis, or 'going' twice	Take three steps in one direction, then three steps back
Six	Roku	Rock and roll (at a push)	A musical genre first popularized in the fifties by Elvis	Either do a silly little dance (if this is not too embarrassing), or do the Elvis lip and wiggle your pelvis
Seven	Shichi	Shi-chi	Sneezing twice	Sneeze twice, covering your mouth as you are doing so
Eight	Hachi	Hat-chi	Hat (with a chi on the end)	Mime putting on a hat
Nine	Kyu ku	Kyu coo	What it sounds like when doves cry	Flap your wings and coo like a dove
Ten	Ju ju	Ju ju	The abbreviated nickname for a close friend by the name of Julie or Julian or the personal pronoun	Point at the other person with your forefinger, twice (lame, I know, but there is no guarantee there will be a person called Julian or Julie in the room).

It's worth giving this a try a few times to see if it sticks. You'll find that after a few goes of doing these words and actions you'll know the first ten Japanese numbers off by heart. (I can't say I've found knowing how to say the number eight in Japanese particularly helpful down the greengrocer's in Catford, but you never know when it might come in handy!)

The kinetic

It is utterly natural for us to use our hands when speaking. Kinetic activities, particularly those used to cement language acquisition, are often gestural. As a baby, I was taught an action to go with a word. In the Beadle household in downtown Penge, holding out both your hands and swivelling them at the wrist meant that the food you were so much enjoying had evaporated. You had eaten it. It was 'gone', 'gone', 'gone'. This ritual was repeated after breakfast, lunch and tea, and was, apparently, a major contribution to cordial family relations. On noticing that someone had eaten all our ice cream, rather than launch into inconsolable shrieking, tears and bitter accusations of sibling theft, the junior Beadles would blithely raise their hands and launch themselves into a happy, sonorous chorus of 'Gone, gone, gone', actions and all.

Forty years later, the scene has moved two and a half miles down the road to uptown Catford. The nose, eyes and surname are the same, but this time it is one-year-old Lou singing the 'Gone, gone, gone' song, his hands held out in a celebratory dance, swivelling at the wrist. This helps Lou to maintain a stoical, reflective presence in the face of the appalling fact that he's eaten all his dinner. And this is not the only word that has a movement attached to it: he also accompanies the word 'hot' with his hand held to his mouth; and 'bye bye', as with most kids, is escorted by a wave.

These words, the ones that have actions attached, were the first he was able to vocalize.

If gesture can embed language into the memory of a baby, then its use shouldn't be dropped as soon as children are out of nappies. In class I will often use a technique we call 'the kinetic'. A kinetic is where you take a piece of knowledge or learning that can be summed up in one or two sentences and say it along with a series of self-designed hand or body moves. For instance, 'There are two uses of the apostrophe: one, the possessive; and two, the contractive.' This isn't a piece of information that would get too many kids excited, but it is vital that children know it, and that they aren't turned off the apostrophe either because it looks like an evil, skinny tadpole, or because it's plain dull. To imbue this piece of information with some greater significance for the children I teach, we designed a kinetic to give it some life.

There are two – stick two fingers up at the world
uses of the apostrophe – do the arm-outstretched-wiggly-finger thing from punctuation kung fu, with a *Blubalubaluba!*
one – stick the middle finger up
the possessive – bring your hands together to your chest and cuddle yourself
and two – two fingers up to everyone who hates us again, lads!
the contractive – mime a circumcision.

This is risqué (I always had to make sure before doing this that the head teacher wasn't showing round a group of local dignitaries), but kids love being risqué. Provided the rudeness is not directed at anyone aggressively, I see nothing wrong whatsoever with tapping into their well of infantile silliness if it makes their lessons memorable and fun. A lot of people in the teaching profession disagree with me on this. But, y'know, bollocks to them.

In his book *The Naked Ape*, the English zoologist Desmond Morris listed nine different gestures a politician might make when delivering a speech to conference. Read the following with Tony Blair in mind, and picture him using these gestures:

1 To make a powerful point, clench your fist.
2 To rubbish another's view, cut the air with one hand, palm down.
3 To be forceful, semi clench both fists, leaving the thumb detached from the fist.

4 To make a point precisely, put thumb and forefinger together.
5 To calm your audience, put both hands out straight, palms down, and make three downward moves.
6 When less sure, or asking for help, both palms face up.
7 To disclaim responsibility, claim innocence, or lie, shrug your hands.
8 To get the audience on your side, mime cuddling them with arms outstretched and gently curling inwards.
9 To assert dominance, wag a finger.

Try this at home

You can use Desmond Morris's gestures (and, of course, add to them with some of your own) while reading through a speech from Shakespeare, and asking your child which of them she thinks a character might use to reinforce the point being made. One of you can read out the text, the other can do the actions. This will lead to a more penetrating understanding of the text as the brain brings bodily perceptions to bear on the material.

There is also a desperately important part of the English GCSE course that most kids follow which goes by the name of 'Writing to Advise, Persuade or Instruct'. It poses scenarios like these:

Your best friend is going through a bad time at home and is thinking of leaving home to live in London. Write a letter to your friend in which you try to persuade him or her not to leave.

Your town needs tourists. Write an article for a magazine in which you promote your town and persuade people to come along and visit.

Write an article for your college newsletter, addressed to parents, which seeks to persuade them to be 'greener'. ➜

Set your child one of these essays. Once he has written his five hundred words, ask him to go through it, allocating Morris's gestures at the appropriate points. If the writing is sufficiently persuasive, the gestures should go naturally with the words.

USING THE FURNITURE

One of the more complex and difficult things our children have to learn is English grammar (see chapter 7 for a brief overview if you, the parent, have forgotten the rules). Often the approach to this in British schools can be termed 'death by worksheet'. Teachers will throw at students, often literally, separate and entirely disconnected worksheets for each element of grammar. This is all very well, and probably works just about OK with high attainers, but there are whole rafts of kids who find this topic difficult, and it does not help if it is taught in a manner that would send the liveliest mind fast-a-kip in ten seconds flat. The problem with 'death by worksheet' is that it rewards only those with linguistic intelligence or an auditory learning style; and it's repetitive, unimaginative and unengaging.

Again, I make the point that a variety of kinetic methods will enrich a child's experience of learning, and give him a broader palette of styles with which to activate his memory come exam time.

First, a mantra with which I shamelessly attempt to indoctrinate other teachers, hoping that they'll infect others with this most dangerous and sacrilegious of all educational ideas: 'Chair good. Desk bad.'

Teachers are prone to becoming over-reliant on desks and tables to the point of addiction. If you think back to your own schooling, you'll probably recall desks in straight rows, either in pairs or in complete isolation. In many schools today, it's much the same story. The main function of this is to stop children talking to one another (which never struck me as being a good idea. The teacher is not the only source of knowledge in a room. Quite often he's not even in the top ten cleverest people in there). 'Divide and rule' is many a teacher's slogan.

Teachers can become physically dependent on certain classroom set-ups. It starts off perfectly normal and manageable, but over the years, telltale signs begin to appear. A desk or student out of place can make the teacher twitch, until eventually she is in the midst of a full-blown addiction. Any new idea is greeted with irritation; the prospect of a child standing in a lesson is enough to prompt a cardiac arrest, perhaps even exclusion from the class for the child. It is vital, for some teachers, that desks and the children sitting behind them stay *exactly* where they are at all times.

But kids need to move around in lessons. If their bodies go to sleep, their minds will follow. Desks stop them from moving at all, particularly those in uniform rows. A desk is a surface to write on, nothing more. Its primacy in the British education system is an unimaginative, fear-ridden joke.

Standing on chairs

The chair is a pretty useful tool. It's not just for sitting on. Pile some up in a corner and you've got a First World War bunker, a volcano about to spew, a piece of post-modern art representing the fragility of the human soul. The chair's portability means that not only does it not get in the way of kinetic work, it can be used as a central part of it. Standing on chairs, for example, is fun. Everyone likes doing it, and it can be used to embed more or less any form of learning. It's a good way, for instance, to drum into pupils that they must always use a capital 'I' when referring to themselves in written form. I ask them to stand on their chairs and reach for the ceiling, as pin straight as possible, while repeating the sentence 'I am important, and that's why I am always a capital letter.' This serves not only to embed a rule, but to give kids a chance to scream from the rafters about how important they are.

I've also found the chair is particularly brilliant for teaching kids all about prepositions.

Try this at home

Prepositions are one of the grittiest parts of grammar. A preposition, basically, tells you your position in time or space. Spatial prepositions – 'below', 'above', 'inside' etc. – are more common, temporal prepositions – 'before', 'later', 'after' – more interesting.

To ensure your child never forgets what a preposition is, call out a list of prepositions and ask him to position himself in relation to the chair in order to reflect each preposition. For example, he could stand **on** his chair; sit **by** his chair; go **near** his chair; walk **past** his chair; lie **along** his chair; get **below** his chair; walk **around** his chair; get **inside** his chair; get **offside** of his chair. As you can see, things can get tricky, so award points for imaginative approaches to the intellectual problems your requests present. (You'll probably find that more boys than girls get that last one. Basically, your chair is offside if it is in front of, or level with, the last chair in defence and the goalkeeper. You see, it's a fun way of . . . the offside rule is from football and it's meant to stop goal-hanging . . . and, well, you have to . . . oh, never mind.)

I once used this technique in class while being assessed for the National Teaching Awards by a trio of educational dignitaries. The boys in the class were engaged to the point of ecstasy, lying over, beneath or on top of their chairs. One of the dignitaries sidled up to me and asked, 'It's lovely to see children so involved. Are any of them on the special needs register?'

'Yes,' I replied, 'all thirty.'

The first time I incorporated a similar teaching method into something I was doing in class was for a study of Shakespearean tragedy. Tragedies from that period share a number of things in common: a tragic hero, of high birth, who has a fatal flaw, the result of which is a loss of status. He'll eventually die in a gory death scene, after a moment of self-realization. These are the conventions of the genre, and they are called, unsurprisingly, generic conventions. We sat on our chairs (initially), then said the following words while performing the corresponding actions:

'A tragedy' – slant your head to one side, hands palm inwards towards the ears, thumbs down, and move the hands around in small circles (this is taken from the video of Steps' cover of the Bee Gees song – you pick up some really unpleasant cultural reference points working in a school) – 'features a tragic hero' – stand up, sword in hand, ready to fight the world – 'of high birth' – sit down, and place an imaginary crown on your head – 'who has a fatal flaw' – kneel down and touch the floor – 'which causes him to go from high' – stand on the chair – 'to low' – move off the chair and sit on the floor – 'till he dies in a bloody death scene' – mime dying in an exaggerated, comic manner – 'after a moment of self-realization' – mime the bit in *Tom and Jerry* when a light-bulb appears just above Tom's head (signifying an idea), and accompany this with an impersonation of Homer Simpson: 'Doh!'

It will all feel a bit Geoffrey and Bungle when you start doing this stuff, but throw off your embarrassment and after a while it becomes second nature.

USING DRAMA

Drama is the ultimate kinetic means of learning. Amazingly, it is not on the national curriculum. Often, it sits marginalized in schools, a spindly and undernourished child in the corner – until the often God-awful school play comes round. Now, I am not advocating that the whole world is a stage, and that educational institutions should be churning out precocious children who like nothing better than to break into a chorus from *Annie* whenever some fool gives them the chance to do so. God help me, I've sat through enough school productions of *Bugsy Malone* to last me several lifetimes. But drama's brilliance as a learning method suggests to me that all kids should have at least a grounding in dramatic techniques, as these can be used to illustrate and investigate the curriculum.

Drama is perfect for those jiggy boys or girls in that it doesn't force them to sit at a desk for hours. In all these activities the child gets to stand up, move about and engage his body in the learning. Drama can also be the best means to engage any pupil, from the most academic to the least. Corinne and Akin, whom you will come across again later in the book, were in my first ever form class, and were leagues apart in terms of academic attainment. Corinne was cleverer than most teachers at the age of eleven, while Akin could not tell you the sound of a single letter. But Corinne had as many problems fitting in as Akin. It was through drama that both of them flourished, as it was a realm in which they could forget their established places at the top and foot of the class. Corinne could be playful, and Akin successful. One of them eventually went into a completely different world as a member of the National Youth Theatre.

Most drama lessons are built around teaching a number of what are called 'drama forms'. These can be used as conduits with which to investigate ideas in other subject areas. Sadly, because most drama activities are performed in groups, it can be difficult to translate these for the home environment. However, the following forms – thoughts aloud/monologue and hotseating – are well worth a try in the front room on a dull Sunday morning.

Thoughts aloud/monologue

Thoughts aloud does what it says on the tin: a child, often in role, says what he is thinking. He is put in role in an imaginary scenario, and says one word or one sentence out loud which sums up what he, or the character he is playing, is thinking. The technique can be layered up to produce something more detailed, more complex and more revealing – a monologue.

In the monologue, your child should focus on ensuring he has eye contact with you, his audience; that he uses whatever space there is in the room to its full potential; and that he doesn't get stuck in the same spot, shuffling from foot to foot. As with all kinetic stuff, it is the movement that helps the information to stick. After the first few nervy goes at this, it will get easier, and as I said, it'll become a valuable tool with which to investigate more or less any subject on the curriculum.

The value of this kind of work is that it helps draw out an in-depth response to topics for which the child might not otherwise be able to come up with an articulate emotional response. It develops empathy, too, as it can be used in the study of more or less any subject: your child could be in role as a Rwandan refugee escaping a horrendous situation, or as something more close to home – a striking miner in the eighties, or an arable farmer in the Cotswolds. It can be enormously rewarding to have such a safe forum in which to explore the potential extremes of human emotions, and to become, as a result, more aware of the feelings and difficulties experienced by others. A monologue allows children to vent their rage, their passions; to achieve catharsis in a controlled environment.

The best of these I have ever seen left a whole class awestruck, and completely changed the way the child was seen by his peers. Adrian, the smallest, quietest of boys who had never done much in the way of standing out, was put into a scenario where he imagined himself as a child who had been the victim of some form of domestic violence. He took the monologue as an opportunity to release the pent-up rage that no one, till then, knew he had. He sprang off the chair, lifted it up and flung it (in a controlled manner) across the room, into a wall. Holding himself as tall as he could and puffing out his chest, he paused, before looking into the eyes of each member of the class and delivering the line, in a stentorian voice, 'I am.' After this powerful performance, no one held Adrian to be anything other than a giant.

Try this at home

Give your child a hypothetical scenario, and ask her, 'How do you feel? Give me your thoughts aloud.' She might reply, 'Sad.' Once she has located the emotional core of her character's response in one word, ask her to build it into a sentence. For example, 'I feel sad, because he is gone.' Finally, give her a minute, sitting on the chair with her eyes closed. Inform her she must use this minute to prepare a speech giving detailed responses to the situation she's in. She must come off the chair when delivering the speech, and must therefore spend some of that minute thinking about what moves she might make. At the end of the minute, it helps if your child is given a countdown to the point when she must perform. When you get down to one, she must spring off her seat and walk to the far corner of the room as she delivers her first line. She'll jump out of her chair, bang her fist in her palm, and unleash a torrent of emotion directly into your eyes.

'I am sad, because he has gone. All my friends warned me he was a drug-addicted, sexually profligate, jobless liar, but I loved him, Mummy. I loved him.'

Actually, this is unlikely. It's all a bit nervy the first time you do it, naturally, but what comes out of this kind of work is an in-depth emotional and descriptive response to any subject, even a difficult one.

Hotseating

This is a fairly standard role-playing technique that can be used with little fuss at home. In schools, it is often the teacher who is hotseated. The teacher plays, for instance, the character of Henry VIII, and the class ask questions like, 'Don't you think cutting your wives' heads off was a bit much really?' 'Aren't six wives a few too many?' 'Don't you think you should lay off the pies a bit? You're going to pop if you keep on like that.' It's an imaginative way of dealing with that part of education that revolves around learning facts, as the teacher can actually be relatively didactic without anyone noticing.

It can also be done with a pupil in the hotseat. Everyone is given a few moments to prepare their questions for, say, Adolf Hitler, Nelson Mandela or Lady Chatterley, and the child in the hotseat is given the same time to get in role. The child in role then sits at the front of the class and everyone fires off their pre-prepared questions.

Try this at home

You, the parent, are to be in role as a historical or fictional character. Give your child ten minutes or so to come up with a set of questions, then answer these to the best of your ability. Then get your own back by putting him in role and asking the questions.

Aside from having it demonstrated that Mum or Dad is a laugh and willing to make a fool of themselves, the benefits are twofold. First, your child has to go through the process of researching and constructing the questions, and must therefore focus on and define exactly what information he needs to know on the subject. He then receives more information (provided Mum or Dad has done sufficient research). The other way, where you are the inquisitor, the child may also arrive at a greater understanding of the character's motivations, and perhaps even the pressures he might have been under.

USING SPORT

When in charge of two classes of thirteen-year-old boys in Canning Town, east London, I took them out to play football every Friday during lesson time. I heard rumours from the rest of the staff, which I was happy to promote, that what we were doing was some kind of complex learning game, where the boys would have to say key words before they were allowed to kick the ball. I wish I were that dedicated. We were just playing football. Pretty badly in my case. An asthmatic forty-year-old smoker who attempts to take on a bunch of football-obsessed thirteen-year-olds is asking to be skinned, and that is what happened.

Having said that, we planned the games during lessons, wrote about formations, investigated role models (this was around the time when David Beckham was perceived solely as being a devoted family man and an excellent example for any young person to follow) and wrote voluminous match reports after the game.

Children's love of sport, and their need for physical exercise, is not properly incorporated into the curriculum. Most professional football clubs run some kind of literacy project – I have seen myself how West Ham United's has benefited the local community – but we don't use football, or any other sport, enough in lessons. Surely, any study of statistics that doesn't refer to the league tables that keep kids glued to a version of reading on a Sunday morning is one that is missing out on a great potential resource. Sports results are algebra; snooker angles, trigonometry; Ronaldinho in flight, pure poetry. Football is not, as some would have it, a thug's pastime. It is an art form as valid as any other. An obsession with it shouldn't be discouraged.

When they play sport, kids learn to work together, and that the individual is only as good as the team. They also learn how to lose with grace, and how to adapt their gameplan to avoid losing again. What's more, it's an intrinsic part of British and world culture, a universal language, and like that other universal language, music, it is woefully underused.

One example of how I've been able to use it as a learning method is in teaching the subordinate clause, sometimes known as the 'embedded clause' in classrooms. A sentence will be running on happily from 'A' to 'B' (for instance, 'Jim wore a pair of brown trousers') when a new piece of information suddenly inveigles itself into the sentence, before it gets to the end. 'Jim, because he was excessively nervous, wore a pair of brown trousers.' Now the sentence goes from 'A' ('Jim') to 'B' ('wore a pair of brown trousers'), but 'C' ('because he was excessively nervous') has popped up like a weed in the garden, and slid itself in as a subordinate clause. (Such a clause is *always* parenthesized with commas.)

This isn't always an easy thing to explain to kids, and I couldn't get it to stick with my boys in a classroom environment, so it was out on to the playing fields and out with the footballs.

We split the boys into groups of four, each group with one football. They were asked to name themselves 'A', 'B', 'C' and 'D'. Poor old 'D' was just a stooge, much like a Halifax Town right-back: he'd watch, with his tongue hanging out and dribble on his bottom lip, as the balls flew past him. Before 'A', 'B' or 'C' kicked the ball they had to make up a sentence. 'A' would say, for instance, 'The exceptionally skilled thirteen-year-old maestro, *comma*,' then pass to 'C'. 'C' would receive the ball, deliver a subordinate clause – 'spotting the stupid defender in his path, *comma*' – then pass to 'B', who would announce, 'bypassed him with a Gazza shimmy, *full stop*.' The sentences they created while knocking the balls around – in this case 'The exceptionally skilled thirteen-year-old maestro, spotting the stupid defender in his path, bypassed him with a Gazza shimmy' – were then taken back into the classroom to be written down.

The subordinate clause does indeed throw a kind of shimmy into a sentence, much in the same way that Gazza in his pomp might have thrown one to a lumpen opposing defender. So we came to know the subordinate clause as the 'Gazza shimmy'. The boys did well in their SATs exams, and were instructed just before turning their papers over, 'Don't forget to throw in a few Gazza shimmies to impress the examiner.'

Kinetic learning requires risk-taking, as when it bombs it bombs completely, and a lot of teachers are scared of it. If you've spent a thirty-year career relying on children sitting silent and still in rows behind desks, it takes a giant leap of the imagination and enormous bravery to try on a completely new coat you are sure is never going to suit you. Younger teachers, however, are generally enthusiastic about it as an idea, which I think is good news for the education of the young people who will take over from us.

Whatever one's response to the research into the benefits of kinetic learning, one part of its use in schools is obvious. We were not designed to sit on chairs all day listening to someone else speak, but we expect our children to endure this ordeal on a daily basis. It isn't good for them. We are not pure intellect in spirit form. We have bodies too, bodies which demand to be used. Our education system tends to ignore the existence of anything below a child's neck, but to have it focus solely on this portion of us writes off nine tenths of ourselves. A child's body is as important as his brain, and he has a right to use it when he is trying to learn.

The Talker:
Social Skills

If your child is a social animal who thrives in the company of others, if she is capable of seeing multiple points of view and is intuitive about others' feelings, she will most likely possess a high quotient of inter-personal intelligence. She will be good at getting people to communicate and like working collaboratively in groups. The socially intelligent child has superb social skills and will often use these to smooth over difficulties between others.

Daniel Goleman, the American psychologist whose book *Emotional Intelligence* has, like Gardner's *Multiple Intelligences*, revolutionized the way the world views intelligence, lists five skills which he sees as key to success in life: self-awareness, self-regulation, motivation, empathy and social skills. Of these, empathy and social skills are obviously within the realm of inter-personal intelligence. If your child has these naturally, she is fortunate, but there are techniques you can use to improve empathy and social ability in those for whom it doesn't come quite so easily.

EMPATHY

If you have a friend or relative suffering from a serious illness and you start to develop some of the symptoms yourself, and suspect you may have the same illness, it may be that you aren't a neurotic malingerer. You just have a very deep empathy with that person. Empathy is the ability to put yourself in someone else's place, and to be able to communicate your awareness so that the other person feels understood.

Along with its twin sister, compassion, empathy is the oil of all satisfying social contact, and development of empathy is a prerequisite if your child is to behave in a manner which will see her as successful in social situations. Without an ability to put ourselves into the emotional landscape of others we care not for their feelings and can become brutish. It is a lack of empathy that allows children to become bullies. An empathetic child, on the other hand, will be sensitive to the feelings of others, perhaps to the point of seeming to have an invisible piece of cord that links them to other people's emotional states. That child will know the pleasure of helping and giving to others from an early age. As David A. Levine, author of *Teaching Empathy*, says, 'It's really quite empowering to learn how to help others. It is a natural inclination most of us have, to reach out to someone in need, yet the art form of helping others is rarely taught as a social and relationship skill.'

There is something to like in everyone you meet; you just have to be prepared to look for it. Your children should have this mantra written on their souls. It will ease their path through life and help them to be successful. They should also know that behaviour is dictated by experience; it always has a cause. Some of the children I have encountered in inner-city schools have had more trauma in their lives than war veterans. I've taught children who do not have beds to sleep in, children who have witnessed the murder of family members, and such things inevitably affect how they behave. So, in order to develop empathy, it is vital to understand that other people have fears, worries and difficult lives that will affect them emotionally, and how they behave with others.

I've seen some fantastic examples of empathy in children. The form class I had in my first year as a teacher had the widest range of abilities I have ever seen in a class: students who now have first-class honours degrees sitting next to children with very serious emotional difficulties. Witnessing Corinne (mentioned in the previous chapter), an enormously high achiever, sit with Akin, who'd seen more at the age of eleven than you'd want to see in three lifetimes, patiently sounding out words as she helped him read, taught me early on that the future is safe in children's hands. One of the advantages of inclusive schooling, where children with serious difficulties are taught alongside mainstream children, is that both sides benefit. You can watch the child with the learning or emotional difficulty glow in the warmth of the attention lavished on him by a mainstream student, at the same time as observing the latter's development of social and caring skills as she teaches. It can be an enormously civilizing experience for a class of young people to be taught alongside a girl with Down's Syndrome, for instance. I have never been in this situation without being impressed by the enormous care and gently nurturing concern shown by young people. You see the best of them in such circumstances.

Being allowed to display empathy is also one of the chief joys of being a teacher. One ex-student, Sarah, used her English book to tell me stories of some of the apocalyptic stuff going on in her life, and I'd use the marking to give the occasional comment on how well she was dealing with it all, and how hard it must be for her. The card she slipped on to my desk one day, secretly, contained a message that is now pinned up on my study wall. It says . . . never mind what it says. It's private.

Using poetry and other stimuli to develop empathy

A child's empathetic skills can be developed through reading stories or poems, or first-hand accounts of real-life tragedies (*The Diary of Anne Frank*, for instance). You could also use the television news or events from a reality TV show as a springboard for discussion as to how people feel when they are in difficult circumstances.

Try this at home

Take a poem, any poem, and ask your child to go through it and underline any powerful images or phrases that have particular resonance for her. Then ask her to go to the computer, log on to the internet and perform a Google image search, entering each phrase/word and seeing what comes up. Ask her to select the best image for each one. On Powerpoint, she can then create a slideshow of the images, with each image staying on screen for ten seconds. (If you don't have a computer at home, a stack of old magazines and newspaper colour supplements should provide enough images for her to cut out and stick on to pieces of paper or card.)

Once the slideshow (or collage) has been constructed, watch or look at it together. For each image your child should record one word that describes her emotional response to that image. For instance, 'fear', 'horror', or 'sadness'. This can help her to connect with the poem emotionally, lead her to a new understanding, and, since many poems on the curriculum are about tragic human circumstances, develop empathy.

Using role play to develop empathy

When I am working with newly qualified teachers (NQTs) and we are speaking about behavioural issues, I ask them to close their eyes and take a full minute of quiet contemplation to imagine the worst possible emotional situation a child in their class could be in. They are then asked to boil the child's feelings down to one word, and to share this word. Following this, they build the word into a sentence that describes how the child feels, and then perform a monologue that springs from having located that child's feelings (see the thoughts aloud/monologue section in chapter 2). For example: 'I mean, how would you feel? Where am I supposed to do my homework? We haven't got a table. Dad smashed it when he was pissed. Do you know what it feels like when he comes home from the pub, drunk and angry with Mum? He doesn't like what she's cooked. He hates his job. He hates us. It's scary.' The point of doing this with teachers is to lead them to an understanding that they may be teaching children whose emotional landscape is very different to their own, or indeed to anything they will ever have encountered.

Try this at home

You can use the same exercise I give to NQTs with your own children. Ask them to imagine a situation a classmate was in, boil it down to one word, then develop it into a sentence and finally a monologue, which they can either write or perform. This exercise could also be performed with a character from a play or novel.

We mustn't disregard the importance of role modelling as well as role play. In school, and throughout the passage of their lives, our children will meet many different kinds of people with many different kinds of experience. The first step towards a rounded empathy is to acknowledge and understand that that difference can cause people to behave in ways you won't be able to predict, and that it is always best to try to be understanding. Empathy can also be taught by behaving this way yourself, through being encouraging and giving your child the message that there's almost always something good about other people. Tessy Britton, Director of Thriving, an organization that seeks to teach children the skills of emotional intelligence, says, 'You have to model empathy in how you deal with the kids every single day – not just when dealing with upsets, but also with frustrations when struggling with material, or when feeling defeated. Anything you do or say which acknowledges and understands feelings, regardless of the emotion, is empathy.'

The facial expressions game

How many expressions has a crocodile got? Four: eyes open, eyes shut, mouth open, mouth shut. They're inscrutable beasts, crocodiles. You can never quite be sure what they're thinking. Though it's probably as simple as 'Kill, eat, sleep, kill again'.

Human faces, provided they haven't been nipped, tucked or Botoxed too much, are more expressive than a crocodile's. You can usually tell what humans are thinking by looking at their faces. Though it's more difficult, if not impossible, when you're a man. There's a reason for this: all men are, to a greater or lesser extent, autistic. We are simply not good at guessing people's emotions from their facial expressions. This is the reason we often get into trouble with our female partners for not being able to guess or anticipate how they're feeling. Men have not needed to evolve the same level of empathy as women. As we were off with our mates chasing flesh and cooking up yet another hare-brained scheme that was bound to fail rather than staying at home rearing the children, we didn't have to become too sensitive to the emotional needs of others. Consequently, we have evolved into boorish, insensitive beasts who can rarely tell when other people are upset.

The facial expressions game is a good way of proving this, and simultaneously of developing that empathy muscle. Any woman with a man in her life might want to toy with him by writing down five emotions on a piece of paper. For instance, you might write down 'happy', 'dopey', 'grumpy', 'bashful' and 'pre-menstrual'. Your male counterpart then has to write down five emotions on a piece of paper himself (if he is able to identify three more to go along with 'drunk' and 'angry'). You take your turn first. Make the appropriate facial expressions for 'happy', 'dopey', etc., and see how many he can guess correctly. He then does his facial expressions, and you have your turn at guessing.

You will win. Men are crap at this game. You will easily prove the primacy of the female in empathetic matters.

SOCIAL SKILLS AND NLP

Neuro-linguistic programming (NLP) is a system of behavioural science devised by an American chap, one Richard Bandler, which seems concerned predominantly with building rapport between its practitioners and other people. It has been popularized in this country by the stage and screen hypnotist Paul McKenna, who earlier this year, I thought, gave me his mobile number, only for it to have miraculously disappeared from my pocket by the following morning. Now that's a hypnotist!

NLP has its devotees, and they are passionate about it. I am sceptical. But among all the talk of modalities and sub modalities that I can't begin to understand (Mrs Beadle describes such things as 'party tricks for bores'), there are a couple of tips related to understanding body language in social situations that can make your child more effective socially.

Our body gives us away without our permission. If a person tells you consistently that she doesn't find you at all attractive, all the while touching her hair and tugging her earlobes, you can be pretty sure you've pulled. If that same person crosses the leg nearest you over the other one, so that her pelvic area is turned away from you, you can be fairly certain she's gone off you. If a child protests that he is all right, but at the same time he is, even almost imperceptibly, shaking his head, then it's likely he is not all right and needs an empathetic shoulder.

NLP practitioners suggest that you can build rapport by mirroring body language – discreetly, perhaps at an interval of twenty or so seconds, so that the other person doesn't notice, sit bolt upright and scream at you to stop copying her. And this process isn't limited to body posture or gesture: it can also apply to tone of speech, or to the accent or language used.

One application of this is described as 'pace and lead', which is a technique we've all used unconsciously without ever realizing it had a name. 'Pace and lead' involves going into another's emotional and physical landscape and mirroring it. Think, for instance, of a poor boy being bullied in a playground, his shoulders slumped. It seems to me an instinctive thing to do to mirror his body language, get down on his level, slump your shoulders a bit and adjust your tone of voice as you ask, 'What's up, mate?' This is the 'pace' bit. When in his landscape, you stay there for a while, empathizing and maintaining the same body language and tone of voice as him, until such time as you judge it appropriate to bring him out of it. As your body language is now in harmony, you can start to adjust yours so that it presents a more positive front, and bring him with you. This is the 'lead' bit. You'll find he cheers up.

My friend Jean Pascal told me an extraordinary story recently that seems to illustrate the point fairly well. On his way back home after a night out, he witnessed a really quite serious fight. One man was on the floor, obviously in deep distress, being kicked witless by two others. Jean Pascal has no experience in the realms of physical violence, but knew enough to be fairly sure that if he rushed in, he was liable to end up on the floor himself with boots raining down on *his* head. So he did something unusual. He sauntered over to the fight and asked one of the attackers what the man on the floor had done. When he was told, he replied in a calm voice, 'That's terrible. I can see why you're angry.' Instantaneously, the two men stopped kicking the other man. Both attackers had effectively been disarmed by the fact that someone appeared to understand why they were doing something so terrible. Jean Pascal continued to talk to them empathetically, in their language, but ever more calmly, and the poor man on the floor soon picked himself up and ran away. Jean Pascal's unconscious use of the pace and lead technique might well have saved a life that night.

I am not for one moment suggesting that you send your children out on to the dark streets on a Friday or Saturday night so that they may practise their skills at empathy. However, you can bring this to bear on your child's experiences in two ways. Firstly, practising it yourself with your children will help you in times of dispute, or when they are upset and are so locked inside that feeling that they can't communicate with you. Secondly, you can teach them the technique. This doesn't mean that they should tour the playground looking for fights so that they can empathize with the victim; but if they are aware of it as a method that they can use with their friends when they are distressed or are struggling, the fact that they are able to demonstrate empathy so easily will ensure that they will keep the friends they have, and be quick to acquire new allies.

Speaking

Most of our social interaction is governed by our use of language, and the predominant way in which we develop social ability is through oracy – which is a fancy word teachers use for speaking fluently.

Oracy can be seen as the fourth 'R', after reading, 'riting and 'rithmetic. Without a fairly practised ability to speak well you'll find that your child's writing isn't much cop. Writing is thought transcribed. Thoughts come in the form of language, internal dialogue, the voice in the head; and if you cannot speak fluently, clearly or imaginatively, then of course you cannot think or write fluently, clearly or imaginatively either. There is stuff you can do at home to ensure that your child is a fluent and interesting speaker, and consequently a better writer.

One of the reasons some children come into their first day in reception class barely able to form a sentence is that with the advent and ubiquity of the television as the sixth member of the family there has been a move away from the shared family dinner around a table towards plates on laps in front of the idiot box. The major part of language acquisition happens before you get to school, and is modelled by parents. All those important skills of discussion, reasoned argument and even humour can be picked up at the dinner table. You get none of it by sitting mute watching cartoons. One of the most important things you can do for your child's education is to ensure that dinner is taken together, around a table.

The actual number of words parents speak to their children is vital to the development of their vocabulary, as Gary Wilson noted in his book *Breaking the Barriers to Boys' Achievement*. Research shows that parents in professional jobs speak, on average, 1,500 more words an hour than those on income support. As a result, a three-year-old from a middle-class family is likely to have a similar vocabulary to an adult from a 'welfare family'. And it's not just the volume of words, it's the tone too. The middle-class parent will utter nine words of encouragement to every word of censure, while the child from the 'welfare family' will receive twice as many negatives as positives. This is obviously going to affect not only their language acquisition, but also their self-esteem.

Try this at home

The dinner table is a place where family concerns can be aired and serious issues raised, but it is also a place to have some intellectual fun. Sebastien (or Bas), Len, Lou and I play several word games as Mummy looks on with that 'Jesus, they're all autistic' glaze. One of these, the 'No you're not!' game, requires the kids to analyse language and make a decision. Dad will go through a list of things he either is or isn't:

DAD: I'm Joanna Lumley.
BOYS: No you're not!

DAD: I'm Jemima Puddleduck.
BOYS: No you're not!
DAD: I'm Huw Edwards, the Welsh newsreader.
BOYS: No you're not!
DAD: I'm Nanny Beadle's little boy.
BOYS: Yes you are!
DAD: I'm a good teacher.
BOYS: No you're not!
DAD: I'm a revolutionary practitioner of experimental pedagogy.
BOYS: No you're not! You just think you are.

You get the point, I hope. As Lou is only one, he hasn't really engaged in the cognitive process part of it. But he enjoys the shouting.

Another game, 'Odd One Out', is used in schools as a cognitive warm-up or starter activity. It prompts kids to make connections between things that might otherwise appear disparate, and to express these connections in language.

DAD: What's the odd one out of a duck, a zebra and a tractor?
BAS: The duck, because the others are quadrupeds.
DAD: Smart lad. Why would it be the tractor?
BAS: Because the other two are animals.
DAD: Double smart lad. And why would it be the zebra?
BAS: Because you wouldn't find a zebra on a farm.
DAD: Treble smart lad. Why would it be nothing?
BAS: What?

And the long winter evenings sped by . . .

Why not try asking your child which is the odd one out between a volcano, an earthquake and a tornado? Or between five, eight and ten? Or between Bush, Blair and Brown? Any question you can generate which can have three possible answers will develop your child's thinking skills.

For older kids, this game can have some relation to what they are studying at school. Who's the odd one out between Macbeth, Lady Macbeth and William Shakespeare? I asked this question of a class of boys I was teaching who had been labelled, somewhat euphemistically, as being 'at risk of underachievement'. They had had difficulty engaging with Shakespeare's language, but their responses to this question revealed immediately that this was my fault. There was nothing wrong whatsoever with what was going on inside their heads. I had thought that they would say it was Lady Macbeth, because she was the only female, or Shakespeare, because he was not a fictional character. But no. 'It's obvious,' replied Luke. 'It's Macbeth. The other two are completely over-ambitious.'

The beauty of this exercise is the quality of response it can generate, and how far you can go with it. It makes kids think, and if you use it around the dinner table, it ensures you're not just sitting there masticating like mute bovines, wishing you were in the front room and the cartoons were on.

Talk is the key mode of transmission of all learning. Much of it is structured in schools so that children learn to talk in groups, negotiate and achieve consensus. This can, and should, be the everyday stuff of normal family life. Anything you can do to stimulate this kind of talk at home will improve your child's social ability.

Standard English, accent, dialect and street slang

When training to be a teacher, one of the first things my class and I were taught was this. Since we were to be working in multicultural environments, where many of the kids' first language would be something other than English, we were to respect that first language as sacred. We would show that we held it in the highest esteem by allowing them, indeed encouraging them, to use it in class, by making displays which celebrated it, and by holding it, and their right to speak it, in utter reverence. If you steal someone's language from them, you steal who they are. What our tutors were telling us was that by paying respect to the language a child spoke we would be paying respect to everything she was, to her family, her country and her right to a heritage.

This also applies to whatever regional dialect or local slang your children may speak. It is their heritage, an intrinsic part of who they are. Parents should not make the mistake of telling their kids that there is a proper or a correct way to speak. How they speak naturally is the proper and correct way. It is what they are. And what they are is good enough.

Of course, it can be distressing for parents when their child comes home with his trousers halfway down his backside, limping deliberately and talking like a gangsta rapper. However, aside from calling his mother a blonx batty'd ho (a fat-bottomed prostitute) when dinner's not to his liking, there's not too much wrong with it. Like the music children listen to, you're not meant to like the way they speak. Adoption of a different way of speaking is simply a part of growing up.

It is also part of a long and proud tradition of deceiving your elders. Historically, groups of people, especially adolescents, have adopted different linguistic forms so that people in positions of authority – teachers, parents, coppers – can't understand what they are saying. Jamaican patois was invented to stop plantation owners listening in to slaves' conversation; Romany people speak a form of slang they call 'tumble', where they simply speak back to front – 'yhw tnod ouy ssip ffo ouy yeson dratsab' is a much-used phrase; and butchers employ the same tumble to speak about their customers in front of them. I became fairly fluent in this at the age of thirteen when, as a Saturday butcher's boy, I was taught the word 'kcollip', as in 'The customer is always a kcollip'. In school, kids still speak what we used to call 'ev and g language' or pig Latin ('Thisagev teachagevervagevs avagev fovagoolv' – work it out for yourselves). Like it or not, as a parent you are an authority figure, and your children will deliberately seek out ways of keeping secrets from you.

Where street slang is likely to get them in trouble is during an oral exam or a job interview. When the question 'Why do you want this job?' is met with the answer 'Wha'gwan bredren? Cos I wanna jam during the daytime and juke and juice all dem bitches in the evening', that civil service job is unlikely to go your way. But all you need to tell your child about language is that, like clothing, it must be suitable for the place in which it is used. You wouldn't wear a diver's wetsuit to a dinner party, unless you were doing it for a bet. Likewise, you don't turn up at Windsor Castle effing and blinding, unless you fancy getting home earlier than you'd planned. (This did actually happen to me, but is a whole other story.)

The point of all this is that it's fine for your children to speak a different way in school to the way you expect them to speak at home. Adopting a 'school' mode of speaking is a survival method they need to fit into environments over which you, the parent, and they, the poor little sods who will be teased or even beaten up if they speak in the wrong manner, have little control. However, they need to know that as well as being able to speak like a petit gangster, they must also be able to speak the language (though not necessarily the accent) of the classic BBC newsreader when this is required. Kids need to know that there is a version of English that is used in a job interview, for example, and that if they don't have access to this form of English then it will affect how they are seen and how well they do in life.

This form of English is called Standard English, and it's basically the language you would expect your bank manager to use when he or she is telling you that your overdraft has been suspended.

How to teach Standard English

Standard English, in fact, is best learned at home. We attempt to teach it in schools, but where kids don't have a day-to-day role model to follow at home, it becomes difficult for them to acquire it. Your children will form a sense of what is correct in language, behaviour and moral sensibilities from you first of all. Hearing my son Len's utterance as he grappled with a T-shirt which stubbornly refused to go over his head – 'F***ing shit-arse' – brought this fact home to me clear as a bell.

So take trouble when you are speaking to them, particularly at an early age, to make them aware that in certain environments the fact that they pronounce 'bottle' as 'bo-uhl' and 'water' as 'wahuh' will make people think they are less clever than they are. All children are precious and brilliant, but if they are unable to speak in the mode certain sections of society regard as acceptable they will be at a disadvantage. So be proud of your accent, and let your children be proud of it in turn, but give them the ability to adjust it where necessary. The fact that British society is riddled with antiquated and unhelpful class snobberies might make you angry, and it is indeed a travesty that people's intelligence and ability are often judged on their accent, but it remains the case that it's difficult to get anywhere in the world without being able to speak to those in power in their own language. You can bet your life that they won't be learning yours.

Stuff to make your child talk

Which, of course, sounds a bit like I'm about to go into Nazi interrogation techniques ('Ve haf vays of making you talk'). As a parent, I find there's often an argument for keeping in touch with your inner Nazi, but when speaking to kids I try to bear a couple of maxims in mind.

Firstly, don't patronize. This is particularly important with teenagers. They are investigating ideas and ways of being. The fact that you, as an adult, may well have tried out and discarded such ideas yourself is of little relevance. As far as they are concerned their thoughts and experiences are unique, and this must be respected. You have a responsibility as a parent to allow that experimentation, not write off what a teenager tells you.

Secondly, take them seriously. A healthy dialogue starts with listening (see the final section of this chapter). The easiest way to teach this to your children is to show that you are listening to them. If you are able to do this, you will find that they have interesting things to say, and that you will learn things from them.

It is through talking to your children that you will be able to model how to speak and how to listen. It must, therefore, be something they want to do. Being able to speak in an adult manner to your children will benefit their powers of expression and your family's emotional life. However, asking the child herself for information is often about as useful as a one-legged man in a bum-kicking contest. 'What did you do at school today?' is an impotent question. She'll just reply 'Can't 'member', 'Nuffink', or 'Y'know, just stuff. God, you're so nosey. Why can't you just leave me alone?' It can be like grappling with a bear with haemorrhoids – painful and pointless.

But there are more effective ways of obtaining such information, like starting some form of shared activity together. A game of cards or some help with the cooking will do: that way she gets something out of the transaction – attention. In exchange for the special attention you are giving her, you'll find that, if you are relatively surreptitious with your questioning, information will flow more freely.

Here are a number of games you can play to open the floodgates of conversation with your child. They are designed to improve oracy skills, which will in turn lead to improvements in their written work; but they can also be used to get that stubborn tongue moving, to get past the grunts, single syllables and shrugs and actually have a conversation about important questions such as what your child did at school that day.

Try this at home: Story in a Bag

The Story in a Bag is a great game to unblock the creative tubes.

I used it recently for an after-dinner speech in front of the cookery expert Prue Leith. In my bag were a frozen mackerel, an MBE (fake), a mask, a sword and a ten-pound note. (A tip here: if you ever want to keep a double seat on a packed train to yourself, carry a frozen mackerel in your jacket pocket. Not only is the smell discouraging, it marks you out as a dangerous lunatic who is to be avoided at all costs.) I used them all as props for the story I was telling, which included at one point a famous chef looking rather surprised when a cockney school teacher deposited a (by now thawing) mackerel in her lap and told her, 'Go on, Prue, do something with that, love.'

If your child has a piece of creative writing homework with which she is struggling, pick five objects – any objects, the odder the better – and put them in a bag. Your child then draws them out and constructs a story around them. She tells the story. The idea is that it develops fluency with spoken language and confidence in speaking in front of an audience (you). If she starts with 'I went on holiday and I packed a frozen mackerel, a fake MBE, a mask, a sword and a ten-pound note', slip back into authority-figure mode, tell her that not taking things seriously enough is a form of cheating, and ask her to start again.

A variation of this is to describe to your child a fictional crime scene. 'Your father was found this morning with his head smashed in, seated with his uneaten dinner on his lap' – or something similar. The objects in the bag are all clues to this grisly murder, and they must construct a story around these objects that explains how the murder happened. Here's an example of how things might pan out: 'Mum prefers dinnertimes at the table, where we can all talk; joust with verbal **swords**. She says it is good for us as a family and for the development of our vocabulary to share mealtimes. I can't see how it works. Dad speaks in grunts and prefers to watch re-runs of *Tom and Jerry* with his dinner on his lap. Yesterday evening, after Mum presented Dad with his meal, he complained the fish was frozen. He pulled a **tenner** out of his pocket and said he was going down the working man's café where they didn't serve oily fish and couscous night after night. Mum was livid. She said she deserved an **MBE** for putting up with him, went upstairs, put one of her stockings over her head like a burglar's **mask**, and came back down. She then brained Dad with the **frozen mackerel**.'

Try this at home: Babble Gabble

This is a scream, a fabulous way of injecting a bit of energy into the most tired, listless, ennui-ridden teenager who is supposed to be studying. It is strictly timed. Give your daughter one minute exactly, and ask her to tell you everything she knows about what she is studying as quickly as she can get it out. Once the sixty seconds are up, she takes the watch, and you have thirty seconds to repeat to her – again, as quickly as you possibly can – all the information you remember from what she told you. At the end of this she corrects the parts you've got wrong, or admitted that you didn't quite get.

Try this at home: Think – Pair – Share

This is the basis of much paired discussion in schools, and provided you are prepared to take a really hands-on approach to helping your children with their homework, it can be used profitably at home to generate ideas.

If a topic is proving difficult to crack, or an essay needs some brainstorming, sit with your child and give yourselves three or four minutes to think about the subject individually. Then come together and discuss your thoughts. Two heads are better than one when it comes to solving a problem, and the fact that you have given a formalized structure to your discussion will further develop your child's fluency.

Try this at home: Devil's Advocate

This is a way of structuring a debate that can lead to some interesting written work. Give your daughter a statement that is plainly wrong, such as 'Smoking is a good and socially useful habit', or 'The grammar school system ensured equality of opportunity for the 80 per cent of children who went to secondary moderns'. Then give her five minutes to construct an argument that upholds the preposterous premise.

A derivation of this is very good indeed when used in preparation for a discursive essay, the kind of thing you might get set in a history exam, like 'Discuss whether Enoch Powell's "Rivers of Blood" speech marked him out as a racist'. For the purposes of stuff you can do at home, it is perhaps better to take a title like 'It is better to marry someone you find physically grotesque. Discuss.' You go through a version of the think – pair – share exercise, the shared bit taking the form of a debate. You propose that marrying a monster is a good thing; your child opposes the idea. Following this argument, swap sides. You now think that wedding a witch is silly; your child thinks engagement to an ogre is a fine idea. Not only will this hone her skills in terms of expressing herself in reasoned argument, she will also learn to see things from both sides, and will have a vast array of new ideas with which to construct the essay.

Socratic questioning

Socrates: ancient, dead and Greek. This is probably the limit of most people's knowledge of him. Before I did a bit of research, I went as far as ancient, dead, Greek, bald and bearded, but then I do work in the field of education and am likely to possess superior knowledge.

Socrates was no great fan of what was commonly believed. For him, what people believed was an amalgam of superstition and untested falsehood. He was of the view that every idea, system or belief should be rigorously tested through thorough, logical questioning. That way, the inconsistencies could be highlighted, certain beliefs could be revealed as fraudulent, and we could then, by a process of elimination, only bother ourselves with things that had been revealed to be true.

This kind of approach, where you do not unquestioningly swallow the views and prejudices of your elders, is great, but it can be unpopular with authority figures. Socrates himself was eventually tried and executed for calling into question the gods' role in the loss of a war, having pointed out that it was more likely to do with the generals' battle strategy. As you can imagine, this was not popular with the generals themselves, and he was forced to drink a cup of hemlock – with the inevitable fatal consequence.

One of the key things any teacher worth her salt seeks to engender in her pupils is a questioning attitude. Don't believe everything you read. Ask the right questions, and find things out for yourself. The beauty of the Socratic method of learning is that you lead children to discover the knowledge themselves. Telling a child something, pushing the knowledge in, stifles thought; drawing it out of them, on the other hand, stimulates and rewards it. All children are perfectly capable of coming up with their own reasoned conclusions about any subject, and often you'll find that their ideas, since they've not undergone the complete process of homogenization into the adult world, are more original and – how shall I put this? – better than yours. Next time they ask you a question, instead of giving them the answer (especially if you don't know it), turn it back on them. What do *you* think? Ask them to work things out for themselves.

The questions you use when practising Socratic questioning can be separated into different types:

Questions that clarify. What do you mean by that? What is your point? Could you put it another way? Do you mean this or this? Could you give me an example? Could you explain that? Would you say more about that, please?

Questions that check assumptions. You seem to be assuming something here, but what? Do I understand you correctly? Why have you based your reasoning on this? What are you taking for granted here? Why would someone make the same assumption you've made here?

Questions that check for reasoning and evidence. Could you give me an example? How do you know? Why do you think that's true? What are your reasons for saying that? Are these reasons good enough? What could change your mind on this? What evidence do you have for saying this? Is that evidence good enough, do you think? How would we find out if this were true?

Questions about particular points of view. Are you implying something here? If that happened, what else would happen as a result? Would that necessarily happen, or is it only probable?

Questions that look into implications and consequences. How could we find this out? What is the logical end of this happening? What else could happen?

I've just tried out Socratic questioning with my eight-year-old, Sebastien. He's just started to make his parents cups of tea, and to tell the truth I'd rather drink pond water with two sugars. So, if his tea-making skills need development, what better method of testing the efficacy of Socratic questioning than to check whether it can prompt a change in the boy's practice? I might even get a decent cuppa out of him as a result. The conversation went like this:

> DAD (sits down and tries on a nurturing face): So, Bas, how do you make the perfect cup of tea?
> BAS: Oh, erm, well . . . I don't know. I know how to make a cup of tea, so I guess I can make, maybe not a perfect one.
> DAD: Have you answered the question?
> BAS: Yeah.

So that's that, then. Socratic questioning – a load of rubbish. Seriously, though, you have to persist.

> DAD: How do you make the perfect cup of tea, Bas?
> BAS: You start off by putting water in a kettle. Then you boil it.
> DAD: What makes you think it has to be a kettle?
> BAS: It doesn't. It could be, like, a saucepan on a stove.
> DAD: What would be the difference between boiling it in a kettle and in a saucepan?
> BAS: You couldn't tell how much water you needed in a saucepan, and you wouldn't know when to stop boiling it.
> DAD: Why wouldn't you know?
> BAS: It wouldn't go cssshsshcrck tick.

Dad: What happens if you don't boil the water?

Bas: Your cup of tea will be cold.

Dad: What do you do once the water has boiled?

Bas: You put a teabag into it, and then you put as many sugars as the person wants in.

Dad: You put a teabag in the kettle?

Bas: Aargh! No. What you do first is you pour the water from the kettle into a cup.

Dad: Would it matter if the kettle were metal or plastic?

Bas: It doesn't.

Dad: What would happen if you drank directly from a metal kettle after it boiled?

Bas: Without sugar or milk? Hot.

Hardly surprisingly, Bas got bored. His attention wandered. I asked him what we had learned, and, as is his way, he came back with, 'Nothing. You may be the most famous teacher in Catford, but you are also the most boring. Your stuff is boring. I wouldn't read your silly book if I was an adult.'

The conclusion you could draw here is don't try Socratic questioning with eight-year-olds: you'll have a really pointless conversation, and they'll just get huffy and tell you truths about yourself you don't want to face. However, you could argue that learning did take place. We had another conversation the following night, and Bas recalled that you didn't necessarily need to use a kettle, a saucepan would do; that not all kettles turn themselves off; that if you don't boil the water properly you're gonna have a pretty rank cuppa; and that putting your lips directly to a freshly boiled kettle is likely to result in a quick trip to the burns unit.

I've used this technique with older kids in class while teaching Arthur Miller's play *The Crucible* for a GCSE coursework essay. Set in 1692 in Massachusetts, it's about a small, theocratic Puritan community who burn half the population as witches on the say-so of a group of fourteen-year-olds. In order to get my students to understand what the logical end of any theocracy – government by the only religion permitted in a society – is, I used a form of Socratic questioning. They were first allocated one religion each – let's take Rastafarianism, Roman Catholicism and Satanism for the sake of this study – and were then asked to identify the three main precepts of that movement, and, through a process of questioning, checking and clarifying, to reach conclusions about the logical end of any of these religions taking over the world and enshrining those precepts in law. The main precepts agreed on were as follows:

- Rastafarians are vegetarians who don't cut their hair and who smoke a lot of medicinal herbs.
- Roman Catholics believe that any form of contraception which works, abortion and divorce are morally wrong.
- The first precepts of Satanism, as defined by the founder and high priest of the Church of Satan Anton La Vey, are not to be so stupid as to trust the media; try not to be pretentious; and do unto others as you would have them do unto you (I think they nicked this from somewhere . . .).

I asked the students questions that led them to the logical end of each religious faith, if it were applied rigorously and without question to the whole of society. They came up with some illuminating conclusions.

Rastafarianism would mean that all barbers and some scissor-makers would go out of business. This might be OK if we are talking solely about Nicky Clarke, but the local barber is a nice Italian feller and it'd be a shame if he couldn't make a living. There would be no need for farmyard animals, so they would either be slaughtered or left to roam. Children would grow up suffering from vitamin-deficiency problems such as rickets, and everyone would be walking round in a permanent haze, and wouldn't be able to do the washing up (so I've heard). An entirely Rastafarian world would be one in which cows and sheep ruled but everyone would be too stoned to notice. I wouldn't want to live there.

The logical end of Roman Catholicism proved a tad scarier: the birth rate would triple, whole continents would eventually be decimated by the spread of AIDS, and the only safe people would be those trapped in sexless, unhappy marriages. No change there, then.

Satanism, in terms of this Socratic questioning exercise at least, is far more benign. People wouldn't be so stupid any more, so there'd be fewer murders and rapes; some arts programming would be scrapped, and Brian Sewell would be retired. All good, then.

Remind your children, however, that asking too many questions can be irritating. Socrates, for all his brilliance, wasn't clever enough to work out the amount of trouble asking difficult questions would cause him. It's all very well and good calling people to account, but be careful they're not vengeful types carrying big sticks.

Listening

This skill is vital in any classroom environment, and in life itself. If your child has the ability to listen during an interminable two-hour physics lesson while all her classmates are off with the fairies on another trip through the rings of Saturn, then she is less likely to be the object of the teacher's wrath when he screams at his charges, 'Why is nobody listening to me? Gravity is interesting. It is. It really is. You poor, misguided fools.' She is also more likely to pass her physics exam.

At one time or another we've all tuned out while some frowsy old bore at the front droned on and on. The development of decent listening skills can be sold to your children as a very good way of avoiding just such torment. You can try to make them aware that time goes much faster if they are engaged in the lesson. Decent listening skills are a means of ensuring you remain in the moment of any lesson, and don't get caught in the purgatory of drifting off and wishing you were somewhere else.

A good listener in a classroom environment treats listening as a highly skilled mental task. Listening has three distinct elements: hearing, understanding and judging. The information goes in first of all and is recognized as being about a particular subject. It is then processed, and the listener asks herself questions to test her understanding, e.g. 'What does metres per second per second mean? Is it that it speeds up this much each second?' Then she will judge the information. 'Does this make sense? Is this believable?' A good listener will instinctively involve herself in this three-part process. She will be able to focus on what's in it for her, regardless of whether or not she finds the subject or its delivery interesting. A poor listener will tend to focus on delivery rather than content, and any tic in the teacher's delivery will attract her attention before content ever does.

Children's satire of the teacher's delivery can be merciless. One poor teacher I met early on in my career had a terrible problem: a repetitive, nervous clearing of the throat. 'Good morning, cough, 7G, cough, cough. Today we are, cough, learning about plate tectonics, cough, cough, cough.' His class would join in, so that as you walked past his room you'd hear something like the following:

TEACHER: Good morning, cough . . .
7G: Cough.
TEACHER: 7G, cough, cough.
7G: Cough, cough.
TEACHER: Today we are, cough . . .
7G: Cough.

TEACHER: Stop coughing.
7G: [silent]
TEACHER: [looks at class, silently]
7G: [still silent]
TEACHER: [still looking at class, silently]
7G: [still silent]
TEACHER: Cough, cough, cough.
7G: Cough, cough, cough.

This would happen every Wednesday morning – a weird ballet stuck in a time warp.

There are repetitive sniffers in British schools, and compulsive shushers. Many teachers are afflicted with the disease that causes them to start every sentence with the words 'Right' or 'OK'. What is more, they often forget to add anything else to these utterances, so that they find themselves standing in front of the class for twenty minutes continually going, 'Right.' 'OK then.' 'Right.' 'Right.' 'OK.' Meanwhile, hordes of bored children are throwing desks at one another. The worst case of this sort I have seen was a colleague blessed with a very curious affectation, the basically/actually disease. Every sentence would include one or other of these words, often both together. 'Basically, Nelson Mandela was actually black. He was actually in prison for twenty-five years. Basically. And he actually got, basically, very bored.' At times he'd lose the thread of even the most basic of actualities, until such point as the rest of the script disappeared and he'd be standing in front of assemblies lost for words, stringing together reams of basicallys and actuallys with precious little other content between them. 'Basically, actually, you've got to actually, basically . . . actually do some basically – sorry, I mean actually . . .'

Your child will encounter such characters standing at the front of her classes. If she is to get anything at all out of her lessons, she will have to become skilled at focusing purely on content and ignoring delivery. She can also try to listen actively, with her whole body: make eye contact with the teacher, angle her body so that she presents a broad frontal plane to him, nod, frown, smile and sometimes even laugh, when this is appropriate.

The brain works four times faster than the mouth, so the good listener will use this time delay to ask questions of herself about what is being presented. How does this connect with what I learned last week? How can I apply this new information in the assessed piece I've got to write? She might also play games to keep her attention honed: see if she can anticipate what the teacher is going to say next, or anything else that will keep her mind engaged and buzzing with learning.

The listening exercise in chapter 6 on musical intelligence is of use for honing your child's skills in this area. Here is another one.

Try this at home

Read your child a fact-filled passage from a book or magazine for a minute or so. Ask her to sit still while you read, with a neutral expression. She is not allowed to take notes. Then let her sit for a minute, and after this she must identify five salient features of the passage you read her. Any text can be used for this. You could even go so far as to read one of those silly celebrity gossip magazines. It would give you a valid excuse for buying one.

Repeat the exercise, though this time tell her to listen actively, involving her whole body, nodding, smiling and frowning. Give her another minute to process the information, then see if this time her recall of five salient points has been improved by the fact that she was listening actively.

Quoting Jean Paul Sartre is the highest form of pretension. I have actually read one of his books and understood, I think, about two phrases. But the concept from his play *Huis Clos* that 'Hell is other people' is one anyone who has sat in a secondary school staff room will be able to relate to. Unless your child is going to be a completely reclusive best-selling author, and these come along very infrequently, she is going to have to deal with other people. More or less every job advert above the level of plucking turkeys for Christmas asks for candidates who have excellent communication skills. Speaking in an articulate manner will be absolutely key for your child's success in the work environment, but remember, speaking well is only one aspect of communication. The softer skills of listening well and of being empathetic may actually be of more benefit. They will make your child not only a more efficient learner, but also a nicer person to be around, a good friend to those who need her, and a valued and trusted worker to her colleagues. As much as hell may well be other people, heaven is the same.

The Thinker:
Reaching the Inward-looking Child

Your child is a thinker. He may spend much of his time on his own and be perceived by some to be introverted or shy. He is, by nature, reflective, more interested in his internal world than in the chatter and hum of others. He's in tune with the self, examining his own behaviour and feelings. He's independent, and capable of thinking and reasoning to a high level. He might not talk much, though.

THE IMPORTANCE OF SPACE TO THINK

As a classroom teacher you are taught not just to take someone's first answer. Kids need time to consider what they think about things, but in an OFSTED-driven, league-table-infected, hundred-mile-an-hour world, a teacher will often be happy with a sea of hands pointing upwards, all the kids ready to volunteer an answer about which they haven't thought. The teacher will then praise that unformed answer, and everyone leaves the classroom reasonably happy, unaware (or not caring) that they have all been talking complete codswallop for fifty minutes.

We don't value tranquillity in classrooms. The temptation is to be all-singing and all-dancing. One of my many faults as a teacher is continuing to believe that fevered activity and laughter equate to deep learning. Such things have their place, but so too does encouraging kids to be contemplative. Giving them access to this state is sublimely useful for them in learning and in life, and it is particularly useful for those intuitive, instinctive intra-personal types.

It can be useful to give time and permission to children to do nothing more than just close their eyes and think about something. Anything. Daydreaming is an underrated pastime. All the most profound achievements in my own life have come as a result of having daydreamed something first. If you can't dream it, it is likely that you won't be able to be it. So, telling your child to just close his eyes and think about something specific, or indeed nothing at all, can be a profoundly rewarding activity. It could come in handy before talking about anything with an emotional content – poetry perhaps – or it could simply be used as an exercise in itself, just to prompt him to create an imaginary landscape he can write about.

We don't respect or encourage kids' right to an imaginary world enough in British education. Everything is so driven by results that there isn't much time to devote to articulating landscapes of the mind, and playing around with new experiences. This is a shame. Childhood is a time when we should be allowed a little latitude to explore. With the progressive Japanization of our education system – by which I mean the burdening of both children and teachers with cripplingly unhealthy levels of overwork – this sort of thing isn't cherished, or even allowed, any more.

Learning is an emotional experience, and your ability to learn is affected by your emotional state. Stress is learning's nemesis. This is why shouting at children is always a silly idea, particularly if you are going to shout at a boy child. The teacher who launches into a character assassination of the young man who has failed, yet again, to hand in a piece of homework that wasn't just scribbled off his mate in the two minutes before the lesson, won't put him in a fabulously receptive state for learning; he'll simply engage the boy's 'reptilian brain'.

You have three brains (see, I told you there's no such thing as thick). Your neocortex is the clever one. It performs all the high-order actions, such as speaking, thinking, and attempting to make the lady in the call centre understand that you already know you haven't paid your credit card bill and that receiving a daily automated call to remind you at a time when you're putting the kids to bed really isn't going to help. Beneath this is the limbic system, your mammalian brain, which is cuddly and will happily roll over on to its back and let you tickle its tummy. This governs your emotional state. And lurking underneath that, sunning itself on top of a rock, is your reptilian brain, the brain stem.

Have you ever wondered why it's so difficult to get a cuddle from either a lizard or a teenage boy? It's because their reptilian brain is too often engaged. The reptilian brain is so unemotional that it doesn't even have too much in the way of maternal feelings. Show a lizard its first-born and it'll probably reach for the salt and pepper. It's not the best part of us, the reptilian brain. It controls our baser instincts: chewing, poohing and, erm, screwing. It doesn't consider, it reacts. Shout at a teenage boy and you'll awaken his prehistoric defence mechanisms. No matter how sensitive, poetry-loving and frilly-shirt-wearing his upper brain functions may be, it will be the reptilian brain that kicks in and takes over, and he'll switch into a mode of response which involves either running away or fighting back – the classic 'fight or flight' instinct. So, shout at a child, he'll shout back, and it'll all escalate into a sorry and unnecessary hill of beans which could easily have been avoided if you'd just asked him nicely and reasonably in the first place.

It's the limbic system that teachers are interested in. We use whatever tools we can to help children locate the contemplative, questioning part of themselves. The part that is happy to soak up knowledge. The part that is interested in learning. Put a child in a relaxed yet positive mood and he'll be more susceptible to learning. If you can flood his brain with feel-good hormones, it is of course more likely that he'll feel good about doing what he's been asked to.

THINKING SKILLS

There is a field of educational practice that seeks to teach children the skills of 'critical thinking'. Since 1998, these thinking skills have been on the national curriculum in primary schools, all of which must teach such components. A thinking skills test is also used to differentiate between applicants for Cambridge University.

In principle, this is a fine idea. An education system must be responsive to the times in which it operates. The ownership of a vast library of facts might win you a game of Trivial Pursuit, or even get you to the second round on *Mastermind*, but it isn't going to make you enormously useful to an employer. Employers need young people who are able to think creatively, to solve problems. Thinking-skills components seek to equip children with abilities they may use in their lives and in the work environment. They also seek to provide a structure through which kids can ask questions, or assume different intellectual positions on a subject. As Descartes said, 'It is not enough to have a good mind. The main thing is to use it well.' Thinking skills courses aim to do just that: train children in the use and application of their minds.

The characteristics of a critical thinker are that 'they are honest with themselves, resist manipulation, overcome confusion, ask questions, base judgements on evidence, look for connections between subjects and are intellectually independent'. I've even heard that critical thinking cures baldness, but I wouldn't trust this. Alain de Botton is a quite fabulous thinker, but an irredeemable slaphead.

De Bono's thinking hats

The granddaddy of critical thinking is Edward de Bono. Mr de Bono, like Descartes before him, believes that 'Many highly intelligent people are bad thinkers. Intelligence is like the horsepower of a car. But you can have a powerful car and drive it badly. Thinking is the driving skill with which each individual drives his or her intelligence.'

De Bono's most famous technique is called the Six Thinking Hats, and it is beautiful in its simplicity. He asks you to imagine a person standing at the front of a house, another at the back, and two more, one on either side. The one at the front protests that the house has a door; the one at the back agrees, but thinks it's in a different position; while the two at the sides see only windows. They argue, passionately, for their own view of the truth. Yet if they had all stood together on each side in turn, they would have realized that they were all right!

The thinking hats are a way of seeing the whole truth of any situation. Each hat represents a different stance that can be brought to whatever subject is being studied, and each one is given its own colour.

- the white hat = neutral observer
- the red hat = self-opinionated and emotional
- the black hat = stern and judgemental, logical and negative
- the yellow hat = looks for the positive
- the green hat = creative and looks for new ideas
- the blue hat = takes an overview of all the others' opinions

At first, this may sound like a particularly silly role-play for a bunch of bored-to-tears businessmen on their day off. You can picture them in their pinstripes, a bunch of daft hats on their heads, arguing because two of them wanted the green one. Nevertheless, if you can put your prejudices to one side, de Bono actually has a serious point here. You can apply a hat test to almost any question, and it will aid your clarity of thinking.

Let's try the most fundamental question of all: is there life after death? The white hat (neutral) wouldn't be able to commit; the red hat (self-opinionated, emotional) would say what he believed despite a lack of evidence ('It exists because it exists, right?'); the black hat (stern, logical and negative) would class an afterlife as 'pish, stuff and nonsense'; the yellow hat (positive) would be all for it; the green hat (creative) would be asking whether there is life *before* death as well; and the blue hat (overview) would oversee the squabbling and try to form some sort of consensus, where there is obviously none.

Next time your child has a piece of homework where he is required to investigate and record his thoughts about something – whether or not a poem is any good, if the war in Iraq was justified, or whether his teacher really does own only one suit – going through a thinking hats exercise will lead him to a rounded view of the subject and will give him all the information he could possibly require to write a decent discursive essay.

Ideology cards

This is a method I use a lot in class, but it can also have an application at home, as you'll see. It is a derivation of de Bono's thinking hats which unlocks a really deep level of learning, and doesn't involve expensive trips down the milliner's.

There are a myriad of ways in which you can look at any book, story or historical event. Ideology cards dictate the way you analyse it – i.e., depending on which card you pick, you interpret or re-imagine the story from a different perspective. As a warm-up exercise you could sit down together and re-tell the story of, say,

Little Red Riding Hood from different points of view. Your son could tell it from the wolf's point of view; you could then tell it from Granny's. If that goes well, try to get him to re-imagine it as a feminist tract, or as a Marxist tract. This is pretty challenging, but another excellent brain work-out.

A feminist reading of Little Red Riding Hood might, for instance, refer to the fact that it is poor Little Red and not her absent elder brother who is given the arduous chore of taking the flowers to Granny; that her journey to Granny's is typical of the journey women must take through life, beset with obstacles and wolfish men of bad intent; and that the woodcutter, like all men, doesn't come to the rescue until after she has undergone the trauma of disappearing down the wolf's stenchy gullet.

A Marxist reading might be more likely to picture the wolf as the symbolic representation of capitalism, growing fat off toiling workers such as Little Red, and Granny. The woodcutter, a working man, is of course the heroic saviour, who brings about the wolf's inevitable destruction. Little Red's hood is also the colour of the revolution. Comrade.

You can have fun with this game. It shows up the fact that no one interpretation of a book or historical circumstance is the correct one, and it affords kids insights into other people's views and the fact that they are of as much worth as their own. If your child has run out of ideas or angles for his essay, this is a challenging way of re-engaging him with a text he may have got bored with.

Try this at home

Ideology cards are great for children who are coming up to their GCSEs or A levels: they will throw a new light on whatever they are studying. Photocopy the following section – or, alternatively, just rip it out (I'll deliberately write a load of old rubbish on the other side). Then cut each approach out (it's better if you laminate them first) and when your child is studying any piece of extended writing and is a bit stuck with it, in no matter what subject, shuffle the cards and give him one. This should serve to re-illuminate the text for him, giving him a different means of unlocking its meaning.

You are a **Marxist reader**. You believe that any text is only ever interesting for the way in which it studies the class struggle in society. You will analyse the text for notions of social, political and economic inequality.	You are a **feminist reader**. You believe that any text is only ever interesting for the way in which it studies the gender struggle in society. You will analyse the text for notions of sexism, patriarchism and gender inequality.
You are a **psychological reader**. You believe that any text is only ever interesting for the way in which it displays or analyses the human subconscious. You will make a Freudian interpretation.	You are an **autobiographical reader**. You believe that any text is a direct expression of an author's thoughts about his own life. You will make an interpretation based upon the text as a metaphor for the author's life.
You are a **formalist reader**. You believe that any text is only ever interesting for the way in which it plays with grammar, punctuation and expected form. You will interpret the text according to this view.	You are a **structuralist reader**. You believe that any text is only ever interesting for the way in which it relates to the reader's own experiences. You will make a personal reading.

To illustrate to younger children the importance of acknowledging other points of view, the warm-up exercise I mentioned earlier is effective: retell the story from the perspective of each character. Transforming stories written in the third person to the first person – i.e. changing 'Red Riding Hood walked to Granny's' to 'I walked to Granny's' – is a useful technical skill with language in any case, but it is the emotional aspect to it that makes it of real worth. Telling the story from the wolf's point of view will develop empathy. He was incredibly hungry, and Granny was a terrible pain in the arse in any case. It was an act of mercy, of euthanasia. Besides, what's a poor wolf to do to keep body and soul alive, and to keep the man from the door? Your child could do this exercise for each character in any story.

Philosophy for Children

My mum had a number of sayings when we were growing up. 'You wouldn't find water if you went to a well' was used when we had singularly failed to find the object she had instructed us to retrieve, and was closely (and invariably) followed by 'If it had a mouth it'd bite ya' when she managed to locate the item herself within milliseconds. This would be followed by fevered discussion, during which she'd scream 'If I said it was black, you'd say it was white' when we had the temerity to call into question the validity of her original instructions. They weren't all so mean-spirited, though, Mother's set of Gaelic wisdoms. There's one she coined which had the timbre of a philosophy, which I will be using with my own children when they enter the adolescent realms of heartbreak: 'There's not much that can't be cured by two paracetamols and an early night.' I, too, have coined the odd dodgy aphorism in my teaching career, which I dispense with largesse to newly qualified practitioners. One such is 'There's not much of worth you can't learn from reading Charlie and the Chocolate Factory'.

You could argue that *Charlie and the Chocolate Factory* doesn't have much to say about the co-efficient of latent heat, river meanders or the Fibonacci series. But you would be wrong. You have to heat chocolate if you are going to make a river of it; Augustus Gloop's descent into that river could be employed as some kind of practical demonstration of how sediment builds up to form geographical features; and the Fibonacci series was originally a way of analysing the mating habits of rabbits, which feature skipping around in the Johnny Depp version of the film. It's a ridiculously overwrought analogy, I know, but it illustrates a point: there's loads of great stuff in literature originally written for small children. Charlie was a respectful, family-orientated, honest boy who, like the meek in the bible, inherited the chocolate factory. The fat one also got what he deserved, as did the one who chewed gum, the venal one and the one who watched TV all day. A better lesson in the immutable law of cause and effect I've yet to read.

Reading the *Mr Men* each evening to my four-year-old son is not only a treat for Dad, but also a nightly lesson in morals and behaviour for Len. (Have you read *Little Miss Bossy*? It's a work of surreal genius, and so true to life: though in schools Little Miss Bossy doesn't have to wear a pair of bossy boots, she gets promoted to deputy head.) When they reach the age of eleven, however, the simple moral lessons of the fable and the fairy story disappear from the curriculum. This lack of a moral and philosophical education might be held to account for many of the problems we middle-aged people refer to when tarring the 'Youth of Today' with an envious cross-generational brush.

We tend to think the lessons contained in small children's literature are only for pre-school. Reprising those lessons for older children, though, returns them to the simplicity of the morally absolute world of extreme youth. Things get more complex as we get older, so absolutes such as 'treat other people with respect', 'work hard' and 'be nice to your mum' are worth revisiting lest they get lost in a busy curriculum.

One of the many lessons that didn't make the final cut in the Channel 4 series *The Unteachables* was a piece of what we call Philosophy for Children (P4C). We were reading Maurice Sendak's *Where the Wild Things Are*, in which Max, the main character, is told off by his mummy for being cross and is sent to his bedroom. When he gets there he sails off to a magical, imaginary kingdom where the wild things live, becomes the wildest of them all and joins in the wild rumpus. The book deals with the potentially destructive impact of temper and its transience, and I was using it as an introduction to a discussion of behaviour and what happens to kids when they get angry. One of the kids – who may well have been the brightest of them all, but was excluded on the first day of the camp – complained, 'You're f***ing patronizing us,' which was a fairly intelligent response to being thirteen and being asked to read a book for four-year-olds. I explained that not only was there nothing in it for me to patronize someone as intelligent as him, as he would eat me, but there was some stuff he could probably do with talking about that was brought up by the book. His own anger had come from somewhere and it was getting in the way of him leading the successful life his intelligence suggested he should have. We had a chat after the lesson, and not only did he take the point, I got a sense that he was grateful for having a chance to talk about what were, for him, some pretty heavyweight issues.

This is what Philosophy for Children seeks to do: to give children a structure within which they can think about and investigate the big questions, the kind of questions that are raised in kids' stories. P4C allows children the chance to ask these questions and, after discussing them, to begin on the path of constructing their own morality. The lessons operate according to pretty much the same model every time. They follow a set path: stimulus, questions, connections, discussion.

Stimulus

You read your child a children's story or fable. For this example we'll take the story of the Three Little Pigs.

Questions

The next stage is for the child to generate questions that arise for him out of the story. To get an idea of how this is done, read the story again and see what moral questions you think it brings up. These can be as simple as 'Should you spend all the money you get?' or of a more high-falutin moral or philosophical nature. I've had a bash myself at the Three Little Pigs and come up with several questions which I've separated into the philosophical and the practical:

Philosophical

How does it feel being good when everyone else is being bad?

Does the fact that we are all going to die mean that we shouldn't bother trying hard?

If you don't believe in God or heaven, does that mean it's OK to be bad?

What is jealousy?

Are older people jealous of young people? Is this OK?

When is the right time to ask for forgiveness?

Why do some people seem to enjoy being nasty to others?

Will your family always forgive you, no matter what you have done?

Why does the hard-working brother forgive the other two?

Practical

Why is it important to work hard?

What's the best way to approach a job that looks as if it's too big for you?

Can every night be a party night?

Philosophical questions help children to develop their own moral sense, to begin to form an understanding of what their views on things are. Practical questions are just a sneaky way of getting the 'work hard' agenda in there. As most stories with some form of moral are about rewarding hard work, you'll generally find it comes up.

Remember, though, these are an adult's questions, and adults don't have the same openness of mind and questioning spirit possessed by children. You'll probably find the questions your own child comes up with after reading a story infinitely more intriguing.

Connections

This bit isn't compulsory. It's about drawing out the themes raised in the questions. The students look at the questions they've come up with, and see if they can group or make connections between them. There are many ways they can do this: they could write the questions on a piece of paper and draw lines to link them; colour code them with a highlighter; or put them into a Venn diagram (the intersecting-circles thing you do in maths to put things in sets). The questions now have a theme. My Three Little Pigs questions above could be linked under the following four headings:

1 The effect the existence of death has on our actions
2 Jealousy
3 The function of the family
4 The nature of forgiveness

When you look at it like that, it becomes obvious that the Three Little Pigs is a high-order piece of literature dealing in serious philosophical concepts.

In making these connections, your child is working in his 'zone of proximal development'. This zone is slightly outside his comfort zone, an area where he is stretched and, as a consequence, acquires new understanding.

Discussion

Discussion of issues brought up in stories is the kind of thing that can easily be done around the dinner table. It doesn't just have to be stories, either. *EastEnders*, for instance, routinely covers moral or social issues that could be used as a springboard for philosophical discussion in which you can transmit moral lessons to your children.

In this situation, though, you would pick one of the questions and outline your initial thoughts, perhaps by playing devil's advocate (see chapter 3). 'I think the eldest pig was a sucker for saving his brothers from the wolf.' Then pass it on. 'What do you think? Do you agree?' The next person will come back saying whether he agrees or disagrees with what you have said, and then go on to say why. This develops oracy and reinforces the fact that opinions have to be justified. All exams ask students to use evidence to back up opinion, and this is an excellent, early-stage practice of the discipline. The adult should be able to guide the conversation so that it goes into interesting areas, or draw it back in if it seems to be going somewhere away from the original question – unless, of course, that somewhere is an interesting place to visit, then this is OK. If it goes nowhere, this is OK too. Just start another question.

Performing this kind of exercise regularly will help your child become open to new ideas and interested in discussing them. It will also help him to become more open emotionally, as it develops one of Daniel Goleman's key skills for success in life, that of self-awareness. He will learn this best if you, his predominant role model, show him how to do it by doing it yourself.

Memory tricks

Unavoidably, the education system still requires kids to retain items of knowledge. This method of learning by rote is often satirized, and is felt by educationalists to be out of date. Even in Dickens' time, the point of view that children were empty vessels to be filled with facts was the object of satire. Gradgrind, who stands as a totem for these broadly discredited ideas in *Hard Times*, espouses a view of education we would now recognize as being peculiarly Victorian: 'We hope to have, before long, a board of fact, composed of commissioners of fact, who will force the people to be a people of fact, and of nothing but fact. You must discard the word Fancy altogether.'

Education nowadays focuses more on teaching life skills than on facts – the 'give a man a fish and he'll have a meal; give a man a fishing rod and he'll have the ability to fish for several meals' argument. As much as I have some sympathy with this argument (until such point as the fishing rod breaks, then he'll have a long piece of wood which is of no use to anyone), it seems entirely unreasonable to cast knowledge itself as an ugly, forgotten pariah. There's nothing much wrong with knowing stuff. As Reg Holdsworth once said so memorably in *Coronation Street*, 'Knowledge is power.' Children will always be required to commit discrete pieces of information to memory, and it is useful for them to have strategies to do this. Some of these techniques you've heard of and no doubt used while at school yourself, but they're worth a reminder.

Acrostics

You might remember this strategy – using sayings based on initial letters to remember sequences of information – from recorder lessons at primary school. Every Good Boy Deserves Favours/ Football; or Every Green Bus Drives Fast; or better still, Every Green Bogey's Delectably Fantastic (copyright P. Beadle, c. 1973). From recall, this helped you remember the notes on the lines of a musical stave, though I'm not sure why. I was kicked out of the recorder class in my first lesson for being too creative with acrostics.

Acronyms

This is bunging initial letters together to make a memorable nonsense word. The main one I remember from school is SOHCAHTOA. It is related to trigonometry and stands for Sine = Opposite over Hypotenuse; Cosine = Adjacent over Hypotenuse; and Tangent = Opposite over Adjacent. All I remember of trigonometry apart from this is that it was about calculating the area of triangles, and was hellishly difficult, stupendously boring and utterly f***ing pointless. You could, of course, combine the acronym SOHCAHTOA with an acrostic to make the useless information even more memorable.

Mnemonics

Hellishly difficult to spell, stupendously easy to use. A mnemonic is a saying, poem or phrase that will help you recall certain pieces of information. 'In 1492 Columbus sailed the ocean blue' is one that may have stayed with you from your days at school.

One of the most difficult things to get ingrained in kids' heads is the difference between 'there', 'their' and 'they're'. I've lost count of the number of potential A grade students who have all the skills necessary for high academic achievement, in spades, but continually confuse these three words. Since the word 'their' denotes possession, a mnemonic that may help is 'I in it, I own it'. It's short, it's punchy, though it's often lost on inner-city kids who take 'in it' to mean 'innit?' and get terribly confused. 'I in it [innit], I own it [innit] . . . Innit?'

Using stories

Constructing stories from disembodied pieces of information is a fantastic way of memorizing them. You can use this technique for literally anything you need to remember, whether it's a mathematical formula or a shopping list. You might argue that the objects themselves are good enough visual prompts when you get to the supermarket, but without a list you'll often forget things. As a man, however, I hate going around the supermarket ticking objects off a piece of paper. It makes you look too much the obedient swain in the pocket of the wife, as well as being the kind of incompetent idiot who can't remember ten items in a list.

I asked my four-year-old son Len to come up with ten items for a shopping list. His answers were carrots (1), broccoli (2), cauliflower (3), potatoes (4), ham (5), bread (6), butter (7), cheese (8), mussels (9) and sweetcorn (10). This was fairly surprising as these items in no way reflect the normal Beadle family shop of crisps, DVDs, beer, burgers and chocolate. I think he's picked up some nonsense at school about healthy eating. A story that included all these items might go like this.

Tommy Tarrot (1) [cockney rhyming slang for 'carrot'], the **ham** actor (5) with **cauliflower** ears (3), had several awful afflictions: on his feet there were **corns** (10), and he had haemorrhoids that formed the exact shape of a floret of **broccoli** (2). They flared up whenever it was **taters** (4) [short for 'taters in the mould' – cockney rhyming slang for 'cold']. Poor old Tom. They caused him no end of havoc, and he'd often try and ease the **pain** (6) [said in a French accent: think about it] with either a **bread** poultice (6, again) or by spreading **butter** (7) on them. As a result he developed tremendous **mussels** (9) in his left arm. People spotted this deformity, but rarely would they point it out, as they were too well **bred** (6, again). Ouch – what a **cheesy** (8) pun!

I put bread in the story three times as this is the item I always return home without, to the tune of much scolding.

Trying it out down Catford Tesco the next day, in an attempt, once and for all, to start eating a balanced diet, I found that I was able to remember all the items Len had listed for me without recourse to an idiot sheet, but for some strange reason I couldn't bring myself to eat either the bread or the butter. My mind had also made another strange connection: whenever I'm in Tesco and I think of broccoli my right arm reaches unconsciously and automatically for a tin of Anusol.

There is no idea your child cannot understand. Children's brains have evolved specifically to comprehend the most high-order concepts. Sometimes schools forget this, and talk down to children, which is always a bad idea. Use of thinking skills techniques like Philosophy for Children allows them the freedom to discuss the notion of truth and lies, what constitutes reality, or goodness, responsibility for our own actions, the existence of God and what she looks like, whether beauty is to be trusted, if honesty is always the best policy. These are just the cherries on top of an enormous iceberg, to mix a metaphor. Thinking skills give them the ability to form opinions on everything there is and ever was. Sheesh. And they say education is just about passing exams.

The Dreamer:
Visual Learning

Your child responds to pictures, is excited by colour and may well spend much of her time scanning maps. She can visualize objects easily and imagine outcomes in her mind's eye. She has good spatial awareness and is happier taking in new information by looking at a picture rather than by listening to someone talk. She loves drawing, scribbling, doodling and, especially, daydreaming.

Many of us are predominantly visual learners, processing things visually and simultaneously, and need to see a picture in its totality before we can focus on specifics. Many lessons in schools tend to show children information in small sequential chunks. This can be unhelpful for visual learners.

LEFT BRAIN/RIGHT BRAIN

Theories about the different functions of the left and right hemispheres of the brain, and how these influence learning, have been key to the developments in visual learning over the last couple of decades. Here, in brief, is what you as a parent may need to know.

Your brain is divided into two hemispheres. The left hemisphere operates the right-hand side of the body, and vice versa. These two halves are connected by white matter known as the corpus callosum, through which messages are passed between the two sides of the brain.

A Nobel Prize winner called Roger Walcott Sperry, along with his assistant Michael Gazzaniga, performed experiments in the 1950s with patients who had had their corpus callosum severed, as a result of an operation to relieve epilepsy. This cut the link between their two brain hemispheres, leaving them with what was termed a 'split brain' (which sounds like a euphemism for a hangover: 'I can't come in this morning: I think I've split my brain'). These patients were shown images – for instance, a carrot – with one side of their visual field covered up, and asked what they had seen. 'Nothing,' they'd reply. This is because speech is controlled by the left-hand side of the brain, and as the image was coming only into the right hemisphere and the link between left and right had been severed, there was no way for the brain to pass the information about the image of a carrot it had seen to the speech centre. However, despite the fact that the patient was unable to name the carrot, and would protest he had seen nothing, when given a range of objects on a table and asked to use his left hand to pick up what he had seen he was able to select the carrot with a 100 per cent accuracy. He would still swear blind that he hadn't seen anything, all the while inexplicably brandishing a livid orange vegetable in his fist.

These findings have been the bedrock of much educational theory over the last thirty years. They first brought up the concept of laterality of brain function. According to Sperry in a lecture some years ago, the brain is 'two separate realms of conscious awareness; two sensing, perceiving, thinking and remembering systems'.

The left hemisphere is perceived as dominant, since left to its own devices the right hemisphere is mute and illiterate; and as it is the left hemisphere that controls reading, writing and arithmetic, it seems to be the side you most need in school and in life. The world is run on skills controlled by the left-hand side of your brain. This is not to accuse the right hemisphere of being a dunce, however. The right hemisphere processes form, music and geometry – the skills associated with creativity, with being artistic. Hence the old cliché that left-handed people are more creative.

Left-handed/right-brain dominant people and right-handed/left-brain dominant people process information in different ways. The left-hander is thought to use 'visual/simultaneous' processing, while the right-hander will use 'logical/sequential' thought. When asked to find a needle in a haystack, the left-brain dominant will take the logical approach, going through the stack one straw at a time, while the right-brain dominant will smash the haystack all over the shop so that he can see the whole picture at a glance. There is a pretty good possibility that simultaneous processing will spot the needle glinting on the ground straight away, whereas doing things in a logical/sequential manner will leave you with an empty pair of blistered hands. Slow and steady doesn't always win the race. Sometimes the mad, destructive genius of the right brain trumps it hands down.

If you have a left-handed child and she writes with her whole arm over the page, her hand contorted at a ninety-degree angle like a praying mantis with cramp, this is not only to prevent any smudging of the ink as she writes. There is some research that suggests the right hemisphere controlling the left hand favours arm and shoulder movements over fine motor skills. Left-handed children are writing the way their brain tells them to. Let them.

While the left-brain dominant child is held to be logical, and to like bright light and silence when she studies, the right-brain dominant is stereotyped as being messy, preferring to lie down while thinking, and to listen to music while studying. Basically, the left brain is the organized swot who likes to keep her bedroom tidy and can tolerate sums. Your right hemisphere is your brain on drugs: the long-haired, creative loafer you don't bring home to Mother but who is the one you really fancy.

Here are some other characteristics ascribed to the two hemispheres:

Left-brain function (logical)	Right-brain function (feeling)
Looks at things in detail	Wants to see the whole picture instantly (visual/simultaneous)
Fact-based rather than instinctive: bases things on reality	Imaginative
Controls language	Controls understanding of symbols and images
Is in charge of reading, writing and arithmetic	Is in charge of music, philosophy, art and religion
Recalls the past	Imagines the future
Is practical and safe	Takes risks
Analyses data to get information	Gets it just by looking at it
Looks for order and pattern	Looks at the whole picture
Forms strategies	Is impetuous/spontaneous

Right-brain function is more sexy, of course, but it's left-brain function that gets the trains running on time. Since the world runs on left-brain function, those who have, by nature, a right-brain dominance can find it a difficult and scary place in which to live. Against their natures, they have to learn how to function in a left-brain dominant world, suppressing their natural predilection for anarchy and creativity, putting it in the straitjacket of a suit and tie during work hours and only getting their real selves out at weekends. This will explain why so many people who work in environments that stultify them develop all-embracing passions for creative hobbies.

It can also be the cause of quite major conflict between parents and children, where the parent is left-brain dominant and the child right-brain dominant. One of the most fantastically gifted students I have ever taught – and who has the name with the most syllables of any I've encountered – Oluwafunmilayo (Funmi for short), is a free spirit, scared of nothing. There's no idea she isn't willing to grapple with, and her writing is gorgeously florid. She once described her own rage in poetic form as being 'the purplest of flowers'.

For the launch of Teachers' TV, the broadcaster John Humphrys came into our English class and gave of his best, trying to teach a grammar lesson to a group of inner-city kids. It wouldn't be unreasonable to think that interviewing every major politician of the last thirty years was preparation enough for crossing swords with a fifteen-year-old with particularly scruffy handwriting. However, I don't think Mr Humphrys had ever encountered anyone like Funmi before. She flew into a fevered argument with him, challenging his use of a particularly extended metaphor, describing it as 'pathetic'. Humphrys took it all in good grace, but you could tell afterwards he'd been in a fight.

Funmi is clever enough to challenge the most respected and senior broadcaster in Britain on her own terms. Yet sometimes this wasn't enough for her mum. Mum was also fantastic in her own way, but they were different. Mum was immaculately presented, obviously fantastically well organized, disciplined and truly quite something. She appeared to be classically left-brain dominant, and she thought her daughter's unique talent required a few more specifically left-brain disciplines: cleaner presentation, fewer crossings-out, a slightly less haphazard approach. This was the cause of unnecessary friction between mother and daughter. Mum was asking Funmi to concentrate on things that were of no relevance to Funmi. Funmi was interested in the quality of ideas, in content, in wild flights of fancy. She could not bring herself to take the cosmetic aspects of work too seriously. There was no time in her mind to do the filing, as there was always something more interesting to investigate.

Such an approach brings its problems to those children who adopt it. There are times when you can't hide from it any more, the filing just has to be done. Still, the lesson for parents with right-brain dominant children is to let them follow their hearts. Don't force a child who shows particular talent in, or passion for, the arts into accountancy. Arts subjects can be scary for parents as they don't seem to lead directly to any particularly stable career. It's difficult to make a living as a painter, musician or writer, and most of all we want to keep our children safe. But if music, drama or painting are areas in which they find themselves completely absorbed, then this absorption will lead them to make massive positive efforts, and no positive effort ever goes wasted.

Mind maps

Theories of hemispheric dominance have been used to inform the biggest thing to happen to visual learning over the last twenty years, the mind map. Invented by Tony Buzan, mind maps utilize the theories of brain lateralization to create a visual device which, so it is claimed, will instantly transform your life for the better, help you to make friends and influence people, and, eventually, conquer the world.

Mind maps are effectively a way of taking notes that combines the pictorial and the linguistic. Since the verbal processing centre is lateralized to the left and our visual and symbolic sensibilities are contained in the right hemisphere, by combining words with pictures, we are using both sides of our brain. Buzan claims that this is vastly more effective than traditional forms of note-taking. Orthodox forms of note-taking don't stick in the head, he says, because they employ only the left brain – the swotty side – leaving our right brain, like many creative types, kicking its heels on the sofa, watching trash TV and waiting for a job offer that never comes. Ordinary note-taking apparently puts us into a 'semi-hypnotic trance state'. Because it doesn't fully reflect our patterns of thinking, it doesn't aid recall efficiently. Using images taps into the brain's key tool for storing memory.

Fundamentally, there are two uses for mind maps: brainstorming and note-taking. The mind map gives you a format on which you can free-associate, and record those associations. It can be quite startling how much children actually know about a subject before you teach them (this is called their 'schema'). They may not be aware of the amount of knowledge they already possess, and a mind map is a great tool for revealing this to them. As such, they can be great for kids' self-confidence, serving as huge butterfly nets with which they can capture all their thoughts on a subject.

Since mind maps are a way of retrieving and storing information which is already in the brain, they are fantastic revision tools (see chapter 11). Rather than sitting, head in hands, dribbling over an extraordinarily dry textbook come revision time, get your child to mind map the information she is revising. The fact that it is a creative visual activity means she will find revision a more enjoyable task, and will do more of it. If Buzan's claims are to be believed, she will also recall much more of the information when she gets into the exam room, since she used both hemispheres of her brain to create it.

As a planning tool, mind maps can also be used to collect ideas for an essay. Because the ideas are stored along thematic branches, they are pre-categorized. All your child has to do, having created a mind map as a planning tool, is to number the branches in the order they are to be used in the essay. Their writing simply follows these branches, in order, and the structure is sound.

Mind maps are useful at any age. Teaching a younger child how to mind map gives her a skill she can use throughout her school career. The best example of mind-mapping I've ever seen was by Steven, the son of the lady who runs the local corner shop, whom I was tutoring on a Saturday morning. An exquisitely bright boy, he claimed English was not his best subject. This was somewhat belied by his response to the homework task: to mind map the specific thoughts of Lady Macbeth, using images, as Buzan prescribes, at the end of the lines and writing quotes on the top. The week after this had been set he arrived at our house, precisely two minutes early as usual, carrying a bulky piece of paper, which when unfolded would have covered a football pitch. It was filled with fantastically colourful pictures and brilliant insights. It was quite the most creative piece of work I had ever seen. I asked his permission to put it up in my classroom. It lasted three hours before it lay, in ribbons, on the floor. There are times when working in an inner-city school crushes your spirit.

Once your child has mastered the mind map technique she can use it as a display tool in her bedroom, where it will serve as a visual reinforcement and reminder of the work she has done. Since they look so fantastic, there is a chance she will prefer them to a poster of a doe-eyed, unthreatening male pop star.

The spider diagram

This is a much simpler way of collecting information, and is used regularly in schools. It's less complicated than the mind map and much quicker – the hare of visual techniques to the mind map's tortoise. When time is at a premium and you want to get ideas down quickly, a spider diagram is best. A spider diagram can be used for all the same functions as a mind map, but is less useful for revision as there are no pictures. It is best for capturing ideas quickly, when the brain is working a little too quickly for the hand, and the time-consuming nature of the mind map would mean losing great ideas.

Try this at home

Spider diagrams are as simple as a PE teacher with a hangover. As with the mind map, your child turns her paper landscape, writes the name of the thing she is going to brainstorm in the centre, and then draws four or five lines coming out from this. At the end of each line she writes an idea, and, since ideas breed more ideas, she can free-associate from there.

The never-ending brainstorm

A more interesting variant is the never-ending brainstorm. This is a derivation of the work of Oliver Caviglioli and Ian Harris, who are among the country's predominant experts in devising visual tools for teaching, and it relies on a notion called 'exploding the node'.

As with the spider diagram, the beauty of this particular tool, which gives it a different application to the mind map, is it doesn't have any pictures. With mind maps you can get so engrossed in drawing ornate, detailed pictures of a frog or a pixie that the point of doing the mind map – recording thought – gets lost. It is the never-ending aspect of this tool that fascinates. If you have the stomach to go for the full forty-five minutes – the optimum time, though thirty minutes is fine as a minimum – the ideas generated at the outer ends of the brainstorm are liable to be esoteric and probably – hopefully – vastly original. As guru Sir Ken Robinson says in his book *Out of Our Minds – Learning to be Creative*, 'Creativity is having original thoughts that are of use.' Individual children having original thoughts is not only likely to result in fantastic grades, it is what makes the world go round.

Try this at home

Your child starts off a never-ending brainstorm as she would a simple spider diagram, by turning her paper to landscape orientation and writing a word or phrase in the centre of it. This is the subject about which she will collect ideas. She then takes out six lines from the centre, and at the end of each of these lines she should draw a small circle. This circle is the 'node'. In each of the circles she must write a word relating to the central theme.

Then she 'explodes the node'! This works on roughly the same principle as taking lines off images in a mind map, but this time you take just two lines out of each circle, and put further circles at the end of these. She should put in further words or phrases related to those in the first nodes, take two more lines off these new nodes, and just carry on like this. She'll need to stick pieces of paper on to the initial one to capture more thoughts as they expand outwards. It doesn't matter what a never-ending brainstorm looks like. What is important here is the quality of the ideas generated.

A brilliant exercise to perform at the end of a never-ending brainstorm session is for your child to go through each idea she's had and to cross out anything she's ever heard of, or thought of, before. That way, not only does she consolidate the original thoughts she's had in those forty-five minutes, but she has justified the time spent doing it in a near empirical way. 'In those forty-five minutes I came up with an entirely new and original use for a parsnip, and a fantastic recipe for radish blancmange!'

Fishbone diagrams

Fishbone diagrams are often used in business environments to get to the root of a problem. Basically, they look like a fish skeleton: the problem at hand is written on the 'head', with four 'ribs' drawn sticking out at near perpendicular angles from each side of a 'backbone'. These ribs are then labelled with categories that systematically break down the problem into different causes or aspects of the problem, and the answers or solutions are then written on the relevant bones.

Try this at home

Draw a fishbone as described above, leaving the head on. Ask your child to write down the problem – why am I not succeeding with my homework? for instance – on the fish head. Then ask her to label the four bones with 'surroundings', 'help provided', 'timing' and 'attitude'.

She should record the problems she has experienced on lines coming off each bone. Problems relating to surroundings go on the first bone, to help provided on the second, etc., until such point as the fishbone appears to have a bit of covering to keep out the cold. She should continue to ask 'Why is this happening?' for each sub factor identified, so that the fish appears to regenerate, and to have a more complex skeleton than any fish you might have eaten before.

You are then left with either a solution to your problem – in this case, why your child isn't doing her homework well – or a planning tool for an essay analysing the problem and flagging up potential solutions.

Using images to store memory

The fundamental principle behind all the more advanced memory techniques is the use of images. Our memory works best when we have pictures in our mind's eye to give us something we can visualize when searching for recall. It is through using visual prompts that people manage to commit to memory several hundred numbers in sequence, and then recall them when drunk to the gills.

The loci method

This strange and brilliant technique, borrowed from the Greeks and Romans, involves placing mental pictures of items in specific locations inside an imaginary room, in a specific order. You then imagine yourself walking through the room and seeing all the items you remember in that order. It helps if the images you create are incongruous or wacky, not only because it's fun, but the more striking the picture is, the easier it'll be to remember.

You can, of course, develop your own system. It doesn't have to be a room or a house. It could be a journey you know well: down the road to the shops, for instance, or the journey to school. You can then create images and attach these to parts of your journey. As an example, let's say I need to remember the British prime ministers of the twentieth century in the right order, and I want to use my journey from Catford to school in the East End.

Leaving the door, past number 44, I meet Arthur Balfour, a Scotsman in a kilt; then down the road to number 10 where I see Sir Henry Campbell-Bannerman holding a banner. I get to the bus stop and push back my quiff, noticing that I am standing next to one Herbert Asquith, who asks me what bus stops here.

'The 181,' I reply.

'Does it go past the George?' asks Asquith.

'No,' say I as, by astounding coincidence, along comes David Lloyd George.

We all wait together, then the bus arrives and we jump on. At the back of the bus, craftily smoking a fag, is Andrew Bonar Law, next to his bald mate Stanley Baldwin. I sit away from the smell Bonar Law is generating and unfold my newspaper. The sports pages. It's the World Cup, forty years after England won it under the management of Sir Alf Ramsay.

As I get off the bus in Lewisham, I spot Ramsay MacDonald lurking in a tartan tracksuit on the platform of the DLR station
. . .

You get the point. Linking things to a journey is a great way of remembering them. After a half-hour break from constructing a journey on which all nineteen prime ministers featured, and with no other revision at all, I wrote down all the names I could remember, and managed fourteen. The more outlandish the things that happen on the journey, the better you'll remember.

For me, Ramsay MacDonald wearing a tartan tracksuit lurking around Lewisham DLR station is an image that is likely to stick in the mind for ever.

Rhyme keys

Where the things to be remembered are in a numbered list, you can use rhymes of the numbers as a visual and linguistic key with which to commit the objects to memory. Here is one I've knocked up to help remember the seven intelligences. Here are the rhymes I've chosen:

One – sun (visual)
Two – buckle my shoe (an action – kinetic)
Three – 'To be or not to be' (Hamlet soliloquizing – intra-personal)
Four – a party bore (inter-personal)
Five – jive (musical)
Six – numerical tricks with the number six (mathematical)
Seven – there is no **word** that rhymes, except heaven (linguistic)

Going through the numbers one by one, you come up with an appropriate image to attach to the rhyme.

One – a radiant sun making everything appear bright, visually attractive and colourful
Two – a shoe being buckled by a Year 8 boy
Three – Laurence Olivier playing Hamlet
Four – a social situation, with some awful geezer in a chalk-grey suit yakking about how fantastic he is
Five – Mum and Dad jiving at a wedding to some fifties music
Six – a flashing number six
Seven – you see the **word** in bold to remind you it's linguistic

Drawing a freeze frame

In lessons, a 'freeze frame' is a physical activity involving four or five students. They are given an idea to sum up in tableau form – for instance, the mathematical formula $a \times a = a^2$. The students will be given ten minutes to produce a picture of themselves in tableau, in which they use their bodies to sum up the idea. In this instance, the students might Sellotape a piece of paper with the letter 'a' to their chests. Two would then stand pointing at their watches, to exemplify the 'a times a' bit, and the others would make their bodies into the shape of a square to show the 'a squared' bit.

Try this at home

It's unlikely that you'll have handy access to another three school kids at home, but the process your child will have to go through to think of what picture she would produce if she did have three classmates handy is of value in itself. Using her imagination to move an idea from a book to an abstract picture of how she might physicalize it causes her brain's cogs to whirr at top speed, employing all the creativity she can muster.

Drawing a freeze frame is best done at the end of a swotting session. Ask your child to sum up the most important thing she has learned by drawing the freeze frame she would have created if she had several friends to work with. Once she has completed the drawing, she should present it to you, explaining how the picture she has drawn represents the chief thing she has learned. The complex cognitive task of transferring the concrete to the abstract is the same as if she had actually enacted the freeze frame, and at the end you have a display piece to stick on the wall as a reminder of the learning.

CREATING A LEARNING ENVIRONMENT

The environment in which children learn must be cared for and respected. It is no coincidence that schools with the worst results are often those in the most dilapidated buildings. If a child is taught in a room with hanging ceiling tiles, tatty walls and an assortment of broken desks of different sizes, it's only natural she will infer that her education is not important to people. If children are not sufficiently respected for them to be taught in scrupulously clean, spacious classrooms that are decorated in exciting and innovative ways, it's hardly surprising that some children aren't able to take their education as seriously as we might wish.

No one likes to be cramped or pushed into a corner. I have been very lucky to have worked in a school where there were large, airy classrooms, but I've experienced the other side of it too: teaching in a classroom so small that it was difficult to squeeze the children into it, and everyone had to breathe in if we ever had visitors. The ability level of the students at the second school was higher, but guess which school had the better results and the happier vibe?

So, respect a child's environment and you are also respecting the child. Respect children and they will respect both themselves and you.

It may be that encouraging your child to transform her bedroom into a mini academic Euro Disney has only a minor effect on her educational achievement. Yet there is only one mark's difference between a C and a D, just one mark that differentiates an A* from an A, and this one mark may well be the difference that allows her to go to the university, get on to the course or obtain the job she wants. So if input into your child's immediate environment makes this difference, it is well worth doing in the long run.

A 'language-rich environment' – words on walls

Children pick up learning all the time, sometimes subliminally. If your child's home environment constantly references what she is learning at school, there is a good chance that this will sink into her psyche. So, if your child has been set a spelling test, don't put it in the bin the week after; bung the correct spellings on the wall as a constant visual reminder so that they become second nature through dull familiarity. Putting your child's work up on the wall makes her proud of her achievement, and aware that you, her parents, value it too.

There are hundreds of different techniques for animating a room. Some of them have been discussed in this chapter; you can see many more at work just by visiting a primary school. Some of the best ideas I've seen are easily transferable to the home. Firstly, don't forget the ceiling. A few years ago when teaching *Macbeth* to an all-boys class, we made papier-mâché daggers and hung these from the ceiling with small pieces of string. They looked brilliant. As you entered the room you got a wondrous sense of theatre, and their very presence was a constant reminder of the play and some of its themes. They were also readily available to use as props when reading the play. Sadly, they didn't last too long. Several Year 9 boys enjoyed one fantastic break-time pillaging a group of younger girls with the daggers, before discarding them on the playground floor where they became bloated from soaking up the rain. They weren't much use after that.

But as a principle, this works. It's also a ready reminder of the permanent usefulness of papier mâché and string. You could make masks and staple these to the wall, or create a sort of clothes line on which you can peg your child's work. A piece of string just left hanging from one wall can, again with the help of pegs, make a great display. You might hang up postcards they get from their grandparents and friends.

The world your children inhabit is Technicolor, but much of the teaching they receive may well be in black and white. There is no reason this should be so. A lot of excellent work has been done in primary schools to ensure that the landscapes young children inhabit are visually rich, and some of this has crossed over into the secondary environment, though not enough. Your child may leave a primary school where the walls are a multi-coloured intellectual adventure in themselves and go to a secondary in which neutral paint is peeling off bare walls. As a parent you can circumvent this, to a degree, by ensuring that not only is your child's home environment rich in visual stimuli, but when you are helping her with her homework you always bear in mind the fact that sometimes a picture is worth a thousand words.

If you have to explain something, and you can show it in pictorial form, you will have produced for your child a readily understandable explanation which stimulates the mind's chief mechanism for storing memories. The same applies to her own work. Writing is not the only acceptable method for recording thought. Sometimes a mind map, a painting or a diagram is more appropriate and more interesting to produce. You should encourage your child to ask herself the question 'How would this information best be presented?' before she undertakes any extended or important homework task.

❻

The Musical Child:
Using Rhyme and Rhythm

If your child has the ability to construct complex rhythms, and appreciate nuances in pitch or timbre; if he hears patterns easily, can't get music out of his head and remembers things through rhyme; if he can follow a beat, identify an off-key note and has a marked emotional response to a given piece of music, then he is likely to have been blessed with a high dose of musical intelligence. Howard Gardner believes that musical intelligence carries the most emotional, spiritual and cultural worth. For some people, exposure to it can actually improve the way in which they think, particularly when attempting to solve complex maths problems.

THE POWER OF MUSIC

At the time of writing, my youngest son, Lou, is one and a half. He can't argue for toffee – he can't even eat toffee – but he can produce a pretty accurate approximation of the tune for 'Twinkle, Twinkle Little Star'. He can learn tunes. If babies can learn melodies before they can speak, or even walk, there's got to be a place for it in classrooms.

My own experience of this field was formed during the twenty-odd years I trawled what is charmingly named the 'toilet circuit' as a quite spectacularly unsuccessful musician. I was a singer (of sorts). None of the albums I made caused much of a ripple. Over the space of this twenty-year non-career the combined number of records sold would not have amounted to even a tenth of the Krankies' 'Fan-dabbie-dozy' on the first morning of its release.

I remain a music-obsessive, though, and have made it a mission of mine to try to bring as much of it into the classroom as possible. I listen predominantly to sensitive Americans with acoustic guitars and girl troubles, and they sometimes make their way into lessons. The records, not the Americans. If they did I would shoo them out briskly and tell them to take their silly, maudlin songs away, and that I'd meet them in the bar after school.

Music is a God-given way of altering the emotional state of the listener. You'll recall that the left brain is the organized side, our right brain the creative. The person who is left-brain dominant is a realist: he will accept things as they are. The right-brain dominant is more likely to be a fantasist, off with the fairies, planning some great scheme. The theorists suggest that those who are right-brain dominant actually work better in mysterious ways. (God himself was right-brain dominant.) Some kids prefer to study in half-light and, crucially, work more effectively while listening to music.

I'm not suggesting that teachers should attempt to deliver lessons to groups of kids who are all nodding away blithely to the skittering, tinny rhythms on their iPods. However, an open-minded practitioner wouldn't write off letting students listen to music when they are doing quiet individual work. It's difficult to manage, but if it actually improves performance then it's worth investigating.

So, if your child prefers to do his homework while listening to music, let him. It may be that he is right-brain dominant and it is actually helping him to study. It may be that it makes it all a more pleasurable experience for him, and there's nothing wrong with that. I have vivid memories of listening to Radio 1 in the late seventies while struggling with one of Mr Elliston's interminable history homeworks, which are now forever associated with the sound of Sting's strangulated, tantric, adenoidal cat-whine, with

Dad yelling in the background, 'I don't know how you study with all that row!' It helped, though. If your child needs music to accompany his homework, you should encourage it. Unless he starts listening to Sting records. In which case get him down the doctor's straight away. He may need to be sectioned.

Music as a mood enhancer

Music is a powerful tool for creating atmosphere or affecting the energy of a room. It can put you in either an energized or contemplative state. It can relax and it can excite. In short, it affects how you feel, how receptive you are, and what it is you are receptive to.

One of the ways in which I put bread on the Beadle family table is by providing INSET (in-service education and training) to other teachers. These are training days when the staff of a school get together to learn new stuff that they can use with their classes, and they are the reason why twice a term you have to magic up childcare from somewhere on a day when you had thought the children would be at school. On these days I will often start with a blast of music to wake the teachers up. Many of them will have used the INSET day as an excuse for going out on the lash the night before. They are rarely grateful for being made to listen to heavy metal full blast, but it works. They don't stay asleep for very long. It also serves as delectable revenge for having been forced to take an early night myself.

Try this at home

For a quick five-minute activity, play a song or track and get your child to transcribe the lyrics as they are sung. This requires speed of thought and not a little penmanship. It is a wake-up call to the brain that you are about to have to function at a high level. Even after a minute of doing this you'll find that listening skills have improved immeasurably. Choose a piece of music with decent lyrics that's not too fast. The best lyrics to use are ones you think will strike an emotional or poetic chord with your child.

Among the reams of research that has been carried out into the effect music has on the brain is a theory that certain types of music can improve focus and concentration. The idea is that listening to Bach and other composers of complex music may 'warm up' neural transmitters and actually improve the response of certain brainwaves, particularly those that deal with mathematical calculation. The most well-known research has been dubbed 'The Mozart Effect'. It suggests that you can make your child a certifiable genius purely by playing him short extracts of Mozart's music. Along the same lines are the plethora of silly 'Baby Einstein' videos, which make all sorts of grand claims. (Einstein was supposed to have said that the reason he was so smart was because he played the violin, and listened to classical music.) As the great educationalist Ted Wragg once said to me, these claims are 'bollocks'. The only thing a Baby Einstein video will improve is the bulging bank balance of the company that makes them.

Recognizing the effect of music on mood, some schools have even gone so far as to have classical music played in the foyer – probably, if they're doing their research, by Bach. This is a fantastic idea. I've been to a couple of schools where they do this, and when you enter you get a real sense both of purposeful calm and of the fact that someone is taking care of the whole learner; every path to achievement is being explored. It also serves to extend the kids' cultural palette, giving them access to avenues of enjoyment that might not otherwise be open to them.

So, to recap, music can help enhance your mood, establish a positive atmosphere, energize the brain and focus concentration. There are other uses, too: it can be used to help develop a child's interest in a subject by appealing to his own cultural reference points, for instance, or it can be used to unlock the imagination.

Unlocking the imagination

Music is a stimulus, and it can be used to kick-start many different forms of activity. One good use for it is to inform creative writing.

Any creative writing a child does is good for him. Expressing his inner self, experimenting with language, focusing effort – these things are all positives, and the technique of writing what you hear in a piece of music is a brilliant way of transforming a blank white page into something useful.

Often, kids find it difficult to start. Give them a title, a pen and a blank page, and you may well have a title, a pen and a blank page half an hour later. The fear of failure can be so chastening as to prevent the child from starting his work. Once you're past this, however, the results can be amazing. Simply by asking a class to listen to a piece of classical music and write what they hear, you have a room full of children fully focused on thinking and writing in swoops of fantasy about seagulls crying as the violins sweep, or about Vikings in Valhalla as the cellos come in.

Rap

At the risk of sounding like a groovy geography teacher, there is a particular genre of music listened to by young people that, while it doesn't do much for these aged ears, is a Godsend for the classroom. I'm talking rap.

Now, while I've occasionally had the guts or stupidity to venture the unpopular opinion that hip hop culture has had a markedly negative effect on behaviour and attitudes to learning in inner-city schools – and I maintain that an all-pervasive youth culture which is obsessed with guns, drugs, easy money, misogyny and materialism can have a pernicious influence on some – the form has its areas of brilliance. Eminem, for instance, is a genius wordsmith. The absence of singing is what makes rap so useful in the classroom. Kids who would never dream of writing poetry in class spend their lunchtimes doing just that, experimenting with rhythm, trying to get their poetic thoughts down on paper, searching desperately for a word to rhyme with 'orange'. I've caught some of the more challenging children I've taught red-handed at this. In the time they might usually reserve for taking the mobile phone off a Year 7 kid, they'll be hunched over a piece of paper wrestling with meter and rhyme. The fact that they identify it as rap rather than as poetry is neither here nor there: the discipline and skill required are the same. So, its use is twofold: not only does it reach out to them culturally, it also provides a discipline and a form in which they can experiment with words.

Rap music has its own secret dialect, which developed over the years from African American slang. You'll already be aware of 'bling', meaning 'jewellery', maybe even of 'beef' (a fight). But how many people would recognize a 'biscuit' as a gun? Or the use of the term 'gank' to describe a theft? I've found that teaching kids some of this new vocabulary adds credibility to the venture and gives them some impetus, along with a whole new argot with which they can create interesting phrases and rhymes.

Try this at home

Encourage your child to have a go at writing some rap poetry. There is no limit to the subjects he could rap about: ox-bow lakes, quadratic equations, precepts of esoteric religions, the history teacher's haircut even. It helps if you give him a rap soundtrack to listen to when he is doing it. This will allow him to get into the linguistic rhythms he will have to employ in his own work. It is likely that a well-chosen rap record (check out MC Paul Barman) will introduce him to some choice new language too. There is also a dictionary of rap terms available at http://www.faqs.org/faqs/music/hip-hop/dictionary. This is a useful aid if your child wants his work to have a real gangsta feel.

As an example of how it can be done with an educational topic, here's one which, in *Blue Peter* fashion, I prepared earlier. It's called 'The Preposition/Proposition Rap'.

A simple preposition: it tells you your position,
In relation to the time or to the ground;
It's a sho' nuff equation, which tells you your situation
To the objects below or those around.
Oh, but on the other hand, a proposition's not so grand;
It's not in, above, below, or roundabout.
Well, it sure ain't nuclear fission.
Don't end your phrase with a preposition,
Unless, of course, you're asking someone out!

The point is that he is creating something rhythmic which can be performed, something which will stick in the head, and which he will enjoy doing. It works on the principle of the 'ear worm'. The ear worm is the chorus so naggingly insistent that you can't actually get it out of your head. It stays there, impinging on your psyche for weeks. It's rarely a tune you actually like, either. The fact that music can do this – stick a bunch of words in your head in which you actually have little or no interest – is deeply under-investigated in British education. This is exactly what we are trying to do as teachers, to embed information. Have you ever wondered why you can't remember where you put your keys five minutes ago, yet you can still recall every line of Gloria Gaynor's 'I Will Survive'? That's the ear-worm quality of music. Why every classroom isn't utterly full of it, every lesson, escapes me. It truly is the great untapped path to learning.

Songs to help you learn . . . and remember

There is no limit to the applications of educational songwriting; and you don't have to be able to play a musical instrument.

On *The Unteachables*, the first thing I did was assess the kids' balance of Gardner's multiple intelligences. The results suggested that most of them, while struggling in the linguistic and mathematical areas, were in fact quite bodily and musically intelligent. This doesn't mean that they could sing. But they *enjoyed* singing, and seemed to prefer to take information in through music.

I am an English teacher, and was only required to teach them that subject. Most of the young people had some difficulties with basic grammar, so I wrote three songs: one on adjectives, one on prepositions, and one on commas.

Any noun without a preceding adjective can be described as being a 'naked noun'. Nouns look better when clothed in adjectives. The Naked Noun song was about how to deal with this:

Verse 1
Now the poor old noun was naked:
He didn't have any clothes.
And he got a cold in his big fat bum,
And he got a cold in his nose.
The poor old noun was lonely
With no adjective for a friend,
And he considered noun suicide –
Which is a terrible way for a noun to meet its end.

Chorus

A noun feels dull and boring, and a lonely twit,
Unless you put an adjective in front of it.
And if you think one adjective isn't enough for you,
Don't just use one adjective, you can use two!

Verse 2

So don't spare on the describers.
Never leave a naked noun.
Get his mates the adjectives
To take him up the town.
And if your noun is lonely,
And his life's a living hell,
Dress him up in gorgeous words,
And a pair of pants as well.

The last lines alone should have been enough to have me arrested. I didn't have much time. Or the dog ate my homework. Or something.

Still, it worked well, as did the other songs. 'The Preposition Song' simply featured the repeated line 'What you doing over there?' With each repetition, the children replaced the preposition 'over' with whatever prepositions they could muster themselves: around, up, inside, beneath, etc.

'Commas Before Connectives' was again related to English grammar. There is a secret to getting commas in more or less the right place: the connective. A connective is basically what we used to call a conjunction: it connects two clauses, which might otherwise stand as sentences on their own. For instance, 'Mr Beadle was a teacher' is a sentence. As is, 'He looked stupid playing the guitar'. It's when you join them together to make a longer sentence that you need a connective. 'So' or 'consequently' both work well here. Join the two together to make one sentence, bung a connective in the middle and you have, 'Mr Beadle was a teacher, so he looked stupid playing the guitar.' The learning point here is that in front of the connective there is a comma. The principle of commas before connectives gives kids who might otherwise be classed as functionally illiterate – which is not a nice thing to call anyone – a chance to grasp something that will actually give their written communication wings. Once you can get to Level 5 – the level the system expects you to have reached by the age of fourteen (see chapter 10) – the world's your lobster, and improvements come thick and fast.

It doesn't always work, though. 'And', for instance, is a sticky beggar. He's a connective, but you don't generally put a comma in front of him. 'Because' can cause problems too. Strictly speaking you shouldn't put a comma in front of him, but as we're talking about a principle that children need to apply, I'll usually insist that they apply it, and leave the discretionary element of commas before connectives to more experienced writers.

The song works best when sung in a Rolf Harris accent, while miming or even playing a wobble board.

Verse 1
I am a lonely comma.
I don't know where to go.
People end up putting me, all over the show.
But I've other uses,
If you get the gist.
I ain't just for separating items in a list.

Chorus
Commas before connectives:
It is the golden rule.
If you don't put a comma before because, then you're a blinking fool.
Commas before connectives
Can really do your nut,
So slap a comma on before, then and, so . . . and always before, but.

Verse 2
But I've other uses, which ain't beyond your reach:
I'm often found, hanging around, before you open direct speech.
And my other usage, which is like a work of art,
Is when you put a comma after an adverbial start.

English grammar is not the sort of thing many would consider a decent subject for a song. Likewise algebraic rules, scientific formulae, tectonic plates and the ubiquitous ox-bow lakes. But any subject on the curriculum can be put to music, and if you can sing about it, there's a damn good chance you'll be able to remember it.

Dancing

The best teacher I have seen so far in my career is a lady called Karrine Buffon. She is a French teacher who teaches French, and is quite stunningly talented. The teaching of modern languages in schools is far in advance of all other subjects except for drama in terms of their application of teaching theory. Modern languages teachers use a lot of music. Many of them start their lessons with a call-and-response version of the A, B, C, D song you might have learned as a kid.

A lot of what Karrine does with her students uses the medium of dance. Teaching the imperative tense, for example, involves students following various, fairly simple instructions such as *lève toi* (stand up), *à gauche* (to the left) and *à droite* (to the right). Rather than throw worksheets at the students for them to fill in the gaps in between yawns, Karrine will put on a piece of French reggae music and ask the class to stand up. In time with the music, she'll take them through a series of dance moves with accompanying instructions. '*Lève toi!*' shouts Karrine, and all the students boogie on up. '*À gauche!*' she exclaims, and they'll boogie to the left. '*À droite!*', and they boogie right.

When the children leave Karrine's lessons, they will not, as is often the case with the fill-in-the-gaps-on-the-paper version of learning, instantaneously lose the information. On the contrary, they go off to lunch singing the lesson's content. All these pupils will forever remember how you say 'left', 'right' and 'stand up' in French.

It takes a brave teacher, or a brave parent, to undertake such an exercise. I'm not so much a dancer, more a 'sitting at the side of the dance floor slagging everyone else off while wishing secretly that I had the guts and lack of self-consciousness to do it myself' kind of bloke. My experience of attempting to copy Karrine was stymied by my white man's overbite. But I can see it's brilliant, and that it works.

Music and poetry

In English classes at school, Mr Latham would ask us to listen to the music in the poetry. I never quite got this, and thought he must be mad. Poetry isn't music. It's words. Words on a printed page and a Sting record on the radio are not the same thing.

There is music in poetry, though. Basically, it's the sound of it. Sound comes from a combination of different letters, each of which has its own sonic personality. A 'b', for instance, has a pretty dull, maybe even obtuse sound; an 's' is sensuous, sexy, saucy and a bit of a sly old snake. Poets know about this stuff. They don't just throw words on to a page and hope for the best. They are aware of how to put words together so that the sounds they make in combination are beautiful or ugly, relaxing or jarring, angry or sad.

Try this at home

A good way to start recognizing the musicality of poetry is to come to an understanding of the different sonic personalities of the letters. It is a useful task to go through the alphabet with your child. Make the sounds with your mouth, then ascribe at least three words to describe the personality of the sound each letter makes. An 'a' sound might be 'pained', 'longing' and 'knowing'; a 'd' sound might be 'aggressive', 'belligerent' and 'neanderthal'. There's no right answer, it's your child's perception of these sonic personalities that counts.

To consolidate this knowledge, record the differing personalities in table form, then you can further embed the learning using a visual strategy where you draw the letters in a style that reflects their personality. These drawings could be colourful and your child can annotate them with the words he has recorded to describe their personalities.

Alliteration

The easiest technique to understand is alliteration: repeated consonant sounds that create a musical effect – e.g., the wayward wombat whacked the wallaby. It's useful for children to know that alliteration can also occur in the middle and at the end of words too, as in 'the cackling cracked crow croaked'.

Try this at home

Ask your child to separate the vowels from the consonants in the alphabet, and for every consonant come up with five words which begin with this letter. Then ask him to make a sentence out of them. Examples of how these might read are 'Billy Beaver beats his bum to the Beatles', 'Danny the donkey dated Dora's daughter' and 'Five fish fly flapping over Fulham Broadway'.

Assonance

Assonance, though every bit as simple as alliteration, can be difficult for kids to get their heads around. I've never quite understood why this is, since it's basically just alliteration for vowels. Perhaps it is because those repeated vowel sounds are more often than not to be found in the middle of words, and they're not so easy to spot.

The most famous example of assonance creating music, which has a bearing on the poem's theme, can be found in John Keats's 'To Autumn', which opens like this:

Season of mists and mellow fruitfulness,
Close bosom-friend of the maturing sun;
Conspiring with him how to load and bless
With fruit the vines that round the thatch-eaves run . . .

It's full of 'o's and 'u's (or 'ohs' and 'oos' for the phonetically minded). Think about autumn for a moment. Most of you will think of the fullness of overripe fruit, or the rich colours of fallen leaves. These oh and oo sounds are full and ripe, and possess a kind of autumnal sensuality that puts a sound picture into your head which equates pretty well with our perception of the season.

Try this at home

To teach your child assonance, use much the same technique as for alliteration: find a bunch of words which have the same vowel sound in them and create a poetic sentence out of them – e.g., 'Five knives spinning within winter', or 'Rodney Ontong boings along wantonly'.

It is not enough, though, just to recognize assonance; your child must also be able to say how the sounds of the repeated vowels reflect the meaning. An 'I', for instance, is a spiky, sharp sound, as are the 'knives' in the first sentence, and a sense of the brittle nature of things in winter is mirrored by the thin sound of the repeated vowel. In the second sentence the roundedness of the 'o' sounds means that you get a sound picture of Rodney as quite a wobbly bloke, perhaps with a big fat bum which he keeps showing off to everyone. Ahem.

Onomatopoeia

Words that sound like their action – e.g. boom, kerching, tick-tock – are used to create specific effects all the time in poetry.

Take a pen or a spoon and bang more or less everything you can find (rattling it along the radiator makes a particularly gratifying onomatopoeic noise). Ask your child to verbalize the sound you are making, and enjoy correcting him as he ventures hesitantly 'Erm, bang?' over and over again. A spoon on a glass can make a 'ting'; the aforementioned pen on the radiator can be either a 'rattle' or a 'prang'.

Once you have introduced the concept, drawing a picture is a good way of ensuring that the knowledge is permanently acquired. Ask your child to draw a graphic representation of the word that somehow shows the action it describes and imitates. He might, for instance, want to draw the word 'zoom' coming out of a car exhaust, or the word 'splat' being flattened by an anvil. These drawings can be as detailed and colourful as he likes. A stick man drawn in ten seconds is not the job here. The fact that your child has taken some care and time to produce his best work will help the concept to lodge in his mind.

One of the most imaginative of these I have seen was by Paul, a young feller with behavioural problems and those super-thick glasses you must need really good eyes to see through. Paul's solution to this problem was to depict a naked and, as I recall, rather hairy male arse supported by a pair of equally hairy legs standing over a bucket. The yellow stream cascading into the bucket was spelt P-I-S-S. He also came up with a derivation of this without the legs, and with the bum at a slightly different angle, with the word P-L-O-P going into the bucket. Despite the imagination employed, and the fact that this was the nearest he had ever got to doing a decent piece of work, I decided against putting either of these fine examples on the classroom wall.

Chorus/refrain

Many poems have a repeated motif. This works in the same way as a chorus in a cheap pop song: it puts the lyric firmly into your head, never to be budged. It is enough to point this fact out to your child and for him to be able to recognize them.

Such choruses are often found in the 'Poems from Other Cultures' section of the AQA *Anthology* most sixteen-year-olds have to study at GCSE. Often such poems deal with oppression and slavery. It might be that the repeated motifs are there to replicate the songs slave workers sang to keep their spirits up. Or it might be that they simply ran out of words for the verse and couldn't be bothered to think up any new ones.

Meter

Like music, all poems have a beat. Beat is the regular pulsing underneath the words. Imagine it as the snare drum you might hear on a Motown record. The question in poetry is, how quick is the beat? The natural pace of the poem is called the meter; and this meter is affected by the musicality of the words the poet chooses, and by the subject matter. The meter itself may also have some symbolic significance, which somehow mirrors the poem's meaning.

Try this at home

There is a pretty easy way of finding out what the appropriate meter is for a poem. Read it out loud to several different beats. Either you or your child should first do a slow handclap while the other reads out the poem over the beat. (The slow handclap needn't be perceived as a comment on the quality of the reading.) Try the same activity over a mid-tempo beat, and finally over a quick tempo. The beat over which the reading sounds most natural is the meter of the poem.

Identifying it is the easy part, though. You now have to come up with a decent reason for the meter being at the pace it is. Sujata Bhatt's poem 'Blessing', which has been studied at GCSE level for the last four years (though no doubt it will be off the syllabus by the time you read this), is about a time of drought followed by a burst in a municipal pipe, which occurs halfway through the poem. At the same point in the poem the meter changes from a slow tick to a frenzied quickstep. Why? Because the initial meter replicates the sound of both a dripping tap and time passing slowly. When the pipe bursts, the poem speeds up to mirror the ecstatic reactions of the poem's inhabitants.

The same technique is used in reverse in a poem called 'Island Man' by Grace Nichols (it's in the same anthology). A Caribbean man is pictured in his homeland surrounded by the delights of colour, sea and sand, and the meter is celebratory, jaunty. Then he wakes up to find (in the words of so many Year 7 stories) that 'it was all a dream'. He is actually in London, and as he wakes up, slowly realizing that he'll soon have to travel on the North Circular to a dull office job, and there won't be any swimming today, the meter of the poem slows to a languorous, ennui-ridden crawl.

Rhythm

A brief lesson about time signatures. Most music that we hear operates under the time signature 4/4, which means it has four beats for every bar. This is similar to the way the heart beats, which is why all modern dance music has this time signature. Put on almost any record you've got and tap along. You'll find it goes 1-2-3-4, 1-2-3-4 for the full length of the song.

However, there are other rhythms. A three-quarter beat is waltz time, or a military march. Poets will often toy around with putting the elements of different time signatures in their work.

This is what they mean when they refer to the rhythm of a poem. Rhythm and meter are not the same thing: the meter is the beat itself, the rhythm is how the words skitter over it.

Again, it is not enough just to identify that the poem has a specific rhythm. You must be able to say why the poet went to the trouble of fitting the words over the top so that they created that specific rhythm. How does the rhythm reflect and heighten the poem's meaning?

I found out only recently that punctuation first appeared slightly before the Shakespearean period to help actors read their lines correctly. It was basically a stage direction: leave a second's gap for each comma, two seconds for a semi-colon, three for a colon, and four for either a full stop, an exclamation mark or a question mark (these are joined together under the collective noun 'period').

Try this at home

Seeing punctuation marks as intervals of time makes it possible for us to use beats and percussive effects to explore pieces of writing. First, read this brief extract from *Macbeth* aloud to your child without any punctuation or expression. Try to make sure you run each word into the next, and try to do it fairly fast.

Thou marshallst me the way that I was going
and such an instrument I was to use
mine eyes are made the fools o the other senses
or else worth all the rest I see thee still
and on thy blade and dudgeon gouts of blood
which was not so before theres no such thing
it is the bloody business which informs
thus to mine eyes.

It doesn't make a great deal of sense without the punctuation. It's dull, featureless and incomprehensible. Now try it with the punctuation. For every comma, do one finger click or clap before you start again, two clicks for a semi-colon, three for a colon, and four for a period (full stop).

Thou marshall'st me the way that I was going;
And such an instrument I was to use.
Mine eyes are made the fools o' the other senses,
Or else worth all the rest; I see thee still,
And on thy blade and dudgeon gouts of blood,
Which was not so before. There's no such thing:
It is the bloody business which informs
Thus to mine eyes.

This will work with any bit of writing. When you read punctuation actively, suddenly the meaning and emotion opens up and shines. Adding the rhythmic effect of the pauses causes it to swing a little, to reveal its music and be a much more pleasurable thing to listen to. Moreover, this is a fun paired activity which you can do with your child, laughing as you mess up the number of finger-clicks or claps. Most importantly, it involves superimposing rhythm on to the text. Consequently, there is bodily involvement in the work, and it'll stick in his head.

It is a fundamentally useful thing for your child to know: if he is reading aloud, he should read the punctuation as well as the words. By leaving a second's gap after each comma, and up to four seconds for every full stop, exclamation mark and question mark, his delivery will suddenly become redolent with drama and meaning. Try it yourself with a kids' book.

Rhyme

I am constantly amazed by how difficult it is for some kids to master this. It never struck me as particularly difficult, but I have witnessed very able children struggle with the simplest of rhymes.

Where the vowel sound and any consonants at the end of the word are the same as those in another word, but the start of the word is different – e.g. 'There was a young woman from <u>Ealing</u> / Who had a peculiar <u>feeling</u>' – you have a rhyme.

If your child is writing a poem and needs to find a rhyme, there's a very easy way of doing this. Let's use as an example looking for rhymes for the word 'but'. The end sound is 'ut', so you just go through the alphabet replacing the 'B' with every possible option:

Cut – as in a paper cut

Gut – what you get after too many pies and lager shandies

Hut – where a thing that lives in a hut lives

Jut – as in 'juts out', like Jayne Mansfield's bosom in a tight jumper

Mutt – a scraggy dog

Nut – either what you eat, what you teach, or what's underneath your barnet

Out – interesting. It appears to obey the rules, but still it doesn't rhyme. This is because we are talking about vowel sounds, not the vowel itself.

Put – same as above. Bung another 't' on the end, however . . .

Putt –. . . and it's a different matter: a golf shot.

Rut – what I was in, in the mid nineties

Sut – this doesn't work either, but if you bung an 'l' in there . . .

Slut – . . . it becomes a spectacularly offensive name for a woman. Bung an 'h' in its place . . .

Shut – . . . and you have the opposite of open. An 'm' in its stead . . .

Smut – . . . and you have something in which the aforementioned slut might appear.

Tut – something old ladies do

This system is particularly useful for finding a rhyme for the last line in a limerick. As in,

Jayne Mansfield they once called a slut,
For the way that her bosom would jut
From out of her jumper.
And bumper to bumper,
Boy, the old ladies would . . . tut.

Poems rhyme. Songs rhyme. It is the rhyme itself which helps them to stick in your head and be an 'ear' and consequently a 'brain worm'. There is something innately pleasing and amusing about constructing stuff that rhymes which makes it such a useful thing to use when learning.

Music has an emotional effect on the person who hears it. It evokes memories. Anyone above a certain age will only have to hear Shalamar's 'A Night to Remember' for the sound of teenage parties, the taste of Martini Bianco and the sight of rah-rah skirts to be conjured up. Does the sound of Gloria Estefan remind you of that lost weekend in Bangkok? Perhaps Dolly Parton was on repeat on the occasion of your first broken heart. Whatever the song, there is a synaesthesic link between music and memory. Music is visual; it attaches itself to images from our past. Since images are the key storage mode for memory, the fact that music evokes them means it is a fantastic tool for storing and unlocking what your child needs to remember. You can also use it to heighten your child's joy in learning, and to put him into states that are conducive to it. Music is maybe the best of all legal stimulants, and if we are to get the best out of our children, it should have far greater prominence in their education than it does at present.

❼

The Mathematician:
Shapes and Sequencing

If your child excels in areas that require a logical approach, applying deductive reasoning to locate a solution; if he isn't put off by the sheer size of a task, and has the ability to break it down into small, manageable chunks, then he is likely to have logical/ mathematical intelligence in spades. He will be a list maker, have a head for numbers, and possess a natural aptitude for seeing the pattern in all things.

'Mum, can you help me with my maths homework?'

This features high up on many parents' lists of top ten questions they never want to be asked by their children, somewhere between 'How cheap exactly is an abortion?' and 'Are you sure heroin is that bad for you?' If, like me, you struggle to do long division without your eyes crossing and a dribble of spit forming on your lower lip, you'll be approaching this chapter with fear. Rest easy. The logical/mathematical is not purely the province of the really hard sum. There are good reasons, apart from the fact that I can't add up, that this chapter is not simply a list of suggestions as to how you might help your child with maths.

THE APPLICATION OF MATHS

Maths is a discipline all of itself. It has a stand-alone quality that isolates it from other subjects (with the exception of music) in that it operates with and communicates in a wholly different language system to them. There is little crossover between the language of number and that of word. There have been attempts by the government to force teachers in every subject across the board to include a numeracy-related activity in each lesson, and whole departments have sat in meetings scratching their collective bonces as they've tried to work out the conundrum, what relevance does maths have to using the apostrophe?

These attempts to improve children's skills in maths by having it infiltrate other subjects are well meaning but misguided. It is not the job of an English teacher to waste a class's time counting the words of *War and Peace* when they could be reading them, and the PE teacher who tells his charges that a certain pass would be better if it were played with the body at an exact thirty-five-degree angle is taking his job too seriously. It's in the realms of possibility for teachers to plan such things if they are given time to do so, but ultimately it's a distraction from the real job in hand, another needless box to tick, and it advances children's education in no way at all.

One of the results of the singular nature of the language of maths is that there are children who are utterly fluent in it, but who struggle to master other subjects – Paul, for instance, a student who could work out the most complex algebraic solution, but could barely write his own name. One of the strangest things I have come across as a teacher was the case of Belinda. Belinda was the Head of Maths' star pupil. She was so advanced in the subject that she would have to sit special papers in it all on her own. The Head of Maths once described her as the most gifted student she had seen in thirty years. Belinda's brilliance crossed over into her work in English, for which I was her teacher, in a very strange way. Her choice of words was nothing special, her ideas about the texts we studied were barely above average, but her punctuation was an art form. She approached sentence construction as if it were a mathematical problem to be solved. They would be of such perfect rationalized complexity that they would have caused an Oxford don to drop his bacon sandwich.

The aptitudes possessed by a child who has high logical/ mathematical intelligence can be used to investigate other areas. Remember, it's not just about sums, it's about logic, sequences, shapes and patterns, too.

Psychogeometrics

This is a fascinating example of how mathematical concepts can be applied to other areas. Crossing maths with psychology sounds a little like tap dancing about architecture, but I've tried psychogeometrics, and it throws up not only some interesting ideas, but several accuracies which reverberate with a little too much truth for it to be a complete fabrication. It is, apparently, 84 per cent accurate.

Psychogeometrics were invented by an American lady called Dr Susan Dellinger, who looks as if she irons her hair every morning. It is a system which classifies everyone into one of five personality types according to a preference for one shape over another. Where this is of use for children is in terms of developing their own self-knowledge: being analytical about their own personality type so that they can be reflective about their reactions in certain situations. Anything that can help a child reach a higher level of self-awareness can only be of benefit for his development and for his performance when it comes to learning other things.

Try this at home

Draw a square, a triangle, a circle, a rectangle and a little scruffy squiggle with a pencil. Ask your child to study them and to choose which shape he feels most drawn to. When he has done this, read out the corresponding personality assessment to him and watch him nod ruefully in agreement, marvelling at its 84 per cent accuracy.

If he chose the square, he *is* one. Square lovers are sticklers. They are orderly, dotting every 'i', crossing every 't' and observing correct process in everything. They are interested in how things get done, always on time, and can be unforgiving if others don't show the same concern for the clock. If you marry a square, not much will go wrong, but you may get a bit bored of having your bouts of affection timetabled.

If he chose the triangle, he is an all-ahead, take-no-prisoners, go-getting, born leader of men. Triangle lovers are interested in success, the bottom line, and will generally get what they aim for, often ending up running their own businesses or heading corporations. They can be brusque with others' feelings. It's not that they can't be empathetic, it's just they want results *now*. If you marry a triangle, it'll be passionate, but you'd better be prepared to take a back seat occasionally.

If he chose the circle, he is more interested in relationships than anything else. Circle lovers just want people to get on, and will often provide the empathy that oils the wheels of other's disagreements. They are peacemakers, likely to be family- and home-orientated, good listeners, and interested in ecological issues. If you marry a circle, there will be lots of love to go around, but you may have to provide it on demand.

If he chose the rectangle, he is at a transitional stage. This doesn't mean he doesn't really fit with one of the other shapes; it may be that the shape which draws itself to him a little less than the rectangle is his real personality type. But at the moment he is undergoing some great change. He is at a staging post in life, and is slightly unsure of himself.

If he chose the squiggle, he is the joker in the pack, straight out of left field and likely to be highly creative and high-octane.

Squiggle lovers can be anarchic, preferring fun to anything else, and as a result their huge successes are often matched by equally substantial disasters. They are multi-taskers, often starting fifteen different things at once, and finishing, well, maybe some of them. Squiggles often find themselves working in the creative industries, and if you marry one, prepare yourself for a rollercoaster ride.

Preferences diamond

Another means of using geometric shapes as a learning tool is the preferences diamond. In school, I'll use this at the end of a unit of work as a consolidation exercise with which children can build skills of prioritization, and get involved with thinking about their own learning, which is always useful. It's easy enough to do at home, and is a visual tool with a pleasing, kinetic, hands-on aspect to it, which means it hits two of the three main learning styles. Its applications are endless. Your child could use it to prioritize his workload, or as a revision tool to identify the gaps in his own learning, and then as a springboard for action in terms of filling in those gaps.

Try this at home

Grab a piece of A4 paper and fold it down the vertical axis, then along the horizontal axis. Your unfolded paper now has folds on it which mark out a cross. Using a ruler, join up the points of the cross, and say 'Cor, strewth!' as you notice that you've drawn a perfect diamond shape. Cut off the triangular pieces of paper outside the diamond.

Measure out and mark the points at one third and two thirds' distance along each outer line, and join the marks opposite each other with pencil and ruler. You should now have a large diamond separated into nine smaller diamonds. Shout 'Hoorah!', then ask your child to write down the nine most important things he has learned at school this week, this month or this term, one in each diamond. You can restrict this to a particular subject if you wish. As such, its potential as a revision tool is immense.

Cut up the paper into those individual, smaller diamonds and ask your child to reconstitute the original diamond with the most important thing he has learned at the very top, the next most important on the second row, and so on until you have one poor, forlorn piece of learning sitting at the bottom on its own, shrugging as it is awarded the title of being the least important thing your child has learned.

Optionally, your child can then stick the re-formed diamond on a piece of card and display it as an aide-memoire.

Categorization

Categorization is one of the key life skills a decent education should give you. Without the ability to categorize, you are less efficient. Think, if you will, of your weekly grocery shop. The shopper who bungs his groceries in the bag willy-nilly leaves himself quite a task when he gets home: the toothpaste is in with the ham, the soap's in the same bag as the eggs, and he will have to make more than one trip upstairs to the bathroom. More efficient people will categorize, putting like with like and saving unnecessary trips upstairs.

Categorization is basically putting things in sets, which you may recall is a logical/mathematical skill you learn about in school at a very early age. But thinking disparagingly of this key skill as something for babies would be a bit daft, as the most cognitively challenging part of writing an essay – that of organizing the initial brainstorm into thematic paragraphs – involves a categorization exercise that is only a slightly more sophisticated version of putting objects into sets.

Try this at home

Ask your child to pick two of his teachers and to brainstorm his thoughts about them. Any observation he comes up with is fine. It can be as humorous or as slanderous as he likes. Once he has come up with a couple of pages full of observations, he should place them into the following categories: Appearance (physical characteristics), Dress Sense, Voice, Teaching Style, Discipline and Humour (he may add any fresh categories he is able to summon up himself). There should be at least one observation for each teacher under every category.

Having completed the categorizing activity, he now has the plan, and process, for writing a cohesive comparative essay, as all the information has been categorized under theme. This ability is one of the key skills he'll need when he's asked to compare and contrast in GCSE exams. (For more details about how your child should plan an essay, see chapters 8 and 11.)

Sequencing

Often, being a teacher is much like being a *Blue Peter* presenter: you are expected to be squeaky clean and to live in a world of unadulterated niceness, and you get through a lot of glue and double-sided sticky tape. There is, therefore, something pleasingly destructive about a sequencing activity: you get to cut up loads of pieces of paper, often leaving a quite appalling mess, and then you stuff it all into an envelope, which you give to a child with a suitably mysterious expression.

Sequencing activities can be used in any subject and at any age, but they are particularly useful for late primary age and early secondary age kids (Key Stages 2 and 3 respectively – see chapter 10), when children are learning how to construct a story.

Try this at home

Take a story from one of your child's books, or at least a couple of pages of one, and cut it up. It is best that these are photocopied, as watching you cut up his school books will lead to mild apoplexy in your child, causing him to end up as a goth who will never forgive you for the day that you, in your aged and pitiful state of ignorance, cut up his book. Cut out each separate paragraph, stuff them in an envelope, and seal it.

Once your child has emptied the contents of the envelope on to a table, he will have various pieces of paper spread around in front of him. What he now has to do is to put them in the correct sequence. Here's a rudimentary version as an example:

- They decided that they would live together and accordingly built a cosy and charming home.
- The roof fell in and they died.
- Once upon a time there were two Welsh mice called Terrence and Garreth.

The story doesn't make a great deal of sense in that order, of course; but put these elements in the right order and you have a narrative full of intrigue, dangerous passions and delicious tragedy, which also has an identifiable beginning, middle and end.

In reordering the story – and I hope you have managed to do it without any assistance from teacher – you will have relied on your knowledge of narrative convention. How did you know, for instance, that the sentence in which the mice were named was the first sentence in the story? What are the first four words?

I can't overstate the importance of envelopes in educational activity. Give a child some work to do on a piece of blank paper, and his shoulders will slump. All he can see is a mass of white, which he'll have to struggle to stain with the results of his backbreaking toil. Give him the same work in an envelope, however, and you're handing him a present and an adventure all rolled into one. His reaction to the envelope is the same as a five-year-old's when given one of those chocolate eggs that contain a tiny plastic toy to put together: interest combined with a touch of excitement. Of course, the five-year-old knows in his heart that the eggs are a bit shit, and that the toy will be dispensed with within ten minutes before the baby chokes on it, but that isn't the point. It is the potential of what might be inside that gives children such a rush. It's the same with the envelope: any reasonable human being would be able to predict that it's just a stupid bit of homework, but potentially it could be a passport to delightful, alien worlds; and they'll always open the envelope with a heightened sense of expectation, starting whatever work is inside with a bit of verve.

When students do this exercise with a slightly more taxing text than 'The Heartbreaking Tale of Terrence and Garreth', they also become familiar with paragraph starts and endings, and realize, hopefully, that you shouldn't start them all with the same word. Another pleasing aspect of this is that in order to put the various paragraphs in the correct order you have to read them first. This way you can use subterfuge and guerrilla tactics to make them read something they might otherwise reject. Ask them, for instance, to read a couple of pages on the accession of King Henry IV and they'll just stare blankly at the paper thinking of something else. Put it in the form of a sequencing activity, however, and it's all been read, comprehended and properly ordered before you've had time to butter a piece of toast.

Sonnets

Writing a sonnet may not automatically jump out at you as being a logical/mathematical activity, but sonnets are a poetic form with a particular, near mathematical format, and their complexity and challenge give them the status of a problem to be solved which can keep kids as involved as they would be in solving a sudoku. I have sat and watched a class of inner-city boys feverishly counting syllables, and an experience like that begins to explain sonnet-writing's extraordinary appeal to children as a learning technique.

A sonnet has fourteen lines that are split into four sections: three quatrains (four lines) and a couplet (two lines) at the end. There is a rhyme scheme that dictates which line rhymes with which. The Shakespearean version of a sonnet has the following rhyme scheme: abab, cdcd, efef, gg. The last words of each 'a' line rhyme, as do the last words of each 'b' line, etc. For instance, A – Ate, B – Meat, A – Gate, B – Beat; C – Clear, D – Jam, C – Fear, D – Spam; E – Mind, F – White, E – Find, F – Bright; G – Jack, G – Back.

The part where it becomes a mathematical and linguistic challenge at the same time is that each line has to have ten syllables. This means that any child writing his own sonnet has to get seriously involved in a syllable-counting exercise.

Ask your child to take an object out of his pocket. Then ask him to write a sonnet on it that describes the object along these thematic lines:

- ✏ Lines 1, 2 & 3 – what it looks like;
- ✏ Lines 4, 5 & 6 – what it feels like;
- ✏ Line 7 – its weight;
- ✏ Lines 8 & 9 – what it would sound like;
- ✏ Lines 10 & 11 – on taste and smell;
- ✏ Line 12 – three things it isn't;
- ✏ Lines 13 & 14 – what it might desire.

The sonnet must follow the prescribed rhyme scheme, and must have ten syllables per line, like the example that follows about the unpalatable subject of the snotty tissue in my pocket:

A – Crumpled, festooned with angular creases,
B – Its whiteness opaque, so dirty near grey.
A – Skin, a translucence which age decreases,
B – Brittle as a stem on a rain-strewn day,
C – Which the weather has left stranded, left soaked,
D – Damp, like a tea towel hanging on a line.
C – It's light as the hole through which the sun poked
D – Defeated, all the time crying, 'I'm fine.'
E – Speaking aloud it will talk as it spits
F – Out the taste of the substance it must hold
E – And the smell others, outside, perceive in it.
F – It's not lovely, new, nor yet really old.
G – It dreams of better life, sleep and good food,
G – A pressed handkerchief, refreshed and renewed.

Well, if I was meant to be a poet I'd have lived in a smaller flat and taken to wearing rustic waistcoats. Shockingly, the person who taught me this technique told me afterwards that if you change the impersonal pronoun (it) to he or she, as appropriate, it turns out that the poem you have written is actually about yourself. I need a holiday or a trolley dash down the self-esteem shop.

It can be hellishly difficult, this activity, but if you have a bright child and you want him to experiment with something that's really going to stretch him, knocking up a sonnet will keep him focused on something constructive for ages. It can be used for any subject and is fantastic for extended independent learning.

Timelines

There are a few ways you can bring numbers into any learning experience. You can take the dates involved in a war, for instance, and perform calculations with them. The fact that you have done something with the information will help it embed, and the dates themselves will be easily recalled. For example, adding the last two digits of the beginning and end years of the Second World War, 39 and 45, gives you 84, and 1984 is the title of a George Orwell novel.

Another interesting technique is the timeline, a mathematical tool that also gives visual representation to the topic being learned. I've used this in school, selecting key dates linked to one of the books being studied – dates of the author's birth and death, the date of publication, key historical events that occurred during the author's lifespan – and sticking them up in the school corridor, to scale. So, if the author was born in 1854 and died at the age of forty in 1894, those two years would be separated in the corridor by a distance scaled down from forty metres. The same goes for all the other key dates in the author's life.

I hope by now it's clear that mathematical intelligence isn't just about grappling with really hard sums. Its application is more about using a set of logical thought processes that can be employed in more or less every lesson on the timetable. Application of this type of intelligence can be seen in a child's ability to prioritize, to manage time effectively and to make logical decisions. You don't even have to be spectacularly good at maths to have a decent working mathematical intelligence. It is always worth fostering in your children a logical approach to solving problems, encouraging them to see things in their constituent parts. These are skills that will be of use throughout the lives they will spend outside the walls that, be they physical or temporal, demark their life in school.

The Wordsmith:
How to Write Well

Your child has the ability to use language well – language with which she'll argue, discuss, inform, describe or even entertain. She is articulate, spots puns and irony quickly, and is sensitive to the nuance, order and rhythm of words. She may also ask a lot of questions (damn her) and has a vast vocabulary which she enjoys showing off. She loves reading and will enjoy writing, particularly of the creative variety. There's a strong chance that she's quick to acquire other languages too.

Linguistic intelligence is most easily defined in terms of a child's literacy: how well she reads and writes. But a heightened ability with language – the ability to commune with others' ideas as recorded in books, to either say what is in their head or communicate it in written form – crosses over into every other area of the curriculum. Our school system is built on the bedrock of reading and writing, and unless your child has attained a certain level of fluency in these, she will struggle. If your child writes fluently, she will stand an infinitely better chance of success in exams than if her language stutters. Indeed, unless a child achieves the national average in literacy at the age of the eleven, she will not be able to access the other areas sufficiently well for them to be of any real use.

It is also my own particular passion. There will have been a point in many a young person's life when they became properly interested in the possibilities of existence during an English lesson. At their best, the activities with which we learn about the written word are transcendent. I recall a lesson several years ago, the day after my wife and I went out on our first date, where half of the class were crying at the beauty contained in a single poem, 'It Ain't What You Do. It's What It Does To You' by Simon Armitage. The sight of Debbie, a girl whose usual greeting to the world was rarely much more than a surly shrug, with a tear forming on her lower eyelid as she mouthed, 'That's . . . that's . . . just beautiful,' is an image that will stay with me until death. This is not just the stuff of feeble Hollywood films about suicidal public schoolboys, but an everyday reality in schools in depressed areas, populated by brilliant young people who are prey to lazy stereotyping in the media.

How, then, can you, at home, stimulate the learning of someone who has a natural ability with language, or encourage it in a child who appears to be really struggling?

First, it's probably useful for me to give you some background about the ways in which English is taught in schools. English is separated into speaking and listening (EN1), reading (EN2) – by which they mean not just whether your child can read aloud, but her ability to take something from it, to identify bias and subtext – and writing (EN3). So, if on her report your child is given a grade for EN1, you will know that this is for speaking and listening, not for reading or writing.

Your child will generally study for two GCSEs in English, one in literature and the other in language. The one that counts most towards the schools' league tables is English Language, the duller of the two, so this is the easier one. In truth, the division between the language and literature syllabuses seems narrow. In the GCSE English Language syllabus, for example, pupils are required to study a Shakespeare play and a prose text, and they also have to answer exam questions on poetry. In the English Literature syllabus, they are required to study a Shakespeare play and a prose text, and they also have to answer exam questions on poetry. There *are* differences between them, but the two separate syllabuses seem to have become so interlinked that at points they are indistinguishable.

There is very little chance for kids to get involved in creative writing on the English Language syllabus. There is an ignored, though perfectly reasonable, argument that teaching children how to write their own stories is not only more likely to get them interested in writing, it will also give them a fluency and mastery over language that will be transferable to whatever forms of writing they'll have to use while in employment. But this is swept under the carpet, leaving kids and teachers alike to endure lessons on 'writing to advise, persuade and instruct', which are of little intellectual worth and are no use at all in the real world for which they are supposedly preparation. All and any writing practice, however, is going to help your child become more fluent. Encouraging her to keep a diary, writing letters to Granny, or to Estonian penpals – whatever appeals to her – will really benefit her powers of written communication in the long run.

SPELLING

Of course spelling is important. Decent spelling is a form of politeness, as by spelling things correctly you are asking the reader to do less work. At its worst, poor spelling makes things very difficult for the reader. I heard the tale of a colleague who, while supplementing his paltry teacher's salary by marking exam papers, came across a piece of work claiming that the writer had been studying for his 'chuckyembrosward'. It took him several days of cogitation and much twirling of the sideburns before he was able to work out that 'chuckyembrosward' was, in fact, the Duke of Edinburgh's Award. It can be thankless work, marking exam papers.

However, parents and pupils alike can place too much emphasis on correct spelling. It can have less impact on understanding than you might think. Ut asnt abslutly vitel. U cun spall avery wurd rong und tha reeder wil stull unnerstand wot u hav writen. As a result of children using a form of shorthand to text one another on their mobiles, this standard of spelling is seen all too often. It is nightmarish to open an exercise book and be greeted with this approach to spelling, but I repeat, you can go too far the other way. Correct spelling is so high on the agenda with parents and in primary schools that kids become neurotic about it, and being over-anxious about correct spelling often results in children not doing any work at all, because they are frightened that they will spell a word wrong. Decent punctuation is more intellectually challenging, and more important to your child's writing.

If your child is having problems spelling decently, here are a few tips that might help them.

Look, say, cover, write, check

This is the chief method children use in primary schools. It is used to commit to memory the spelling of difficult words, and is a technique that takes seconds to learn. It has five stages:

1 You look at the difficult word.
2 You say it out loud.
3 You then cover the word up so you can't see it.
4 You write the word yourself.
5 You uncover the correct spelling so that you can check whether you have got it right.

This technique stimulates all three main learning styles, but seems predominantly reliant on visual recall, and is a bit hit and miss for my liking. More reliable are strategies revolving around breaking the word into its constituent sounds.

Breaking down

You break the word down into its syllables, thereby committing smaller chunks of information to memory. You may not be able to spell 'insignificant' from memory, but break it up into 'in', 'sig', 'nif', 'i' and 'cant' and you have a much more manageable way of retaining the information.

Pronunciation keys

This is where you say a word out loud, in the way it is spelled. Sovereignty, for instance, is a difficult word to spell, so you might deliberately mispronounce it as 'so-very-I' while trying to recall the correct spelling, to remember that there is an 'i' in it. Similarly, the 'n' in government might be pronounced loudly whenever you say the word ('government'), or the 'i' in parliament ('par-lia-ment').

Mnemonics

We met mnemonics in chapter 4, and they are a useful way to help you remember spellings. You can, for example, use little phrases or rhymes. Many children spell argument with an 'e' between the 'u' and the 'm'. Knowledge of the phrase 'It is the gum that sticks the argument together' will help them to remember the correct spelling. To spell 'because' correctly, you might use the initial-letter mnemonic 'Big Elephants Can't Always Use Small Exits'. The scope for making up your own spelling mnemonics at home is enormous, and again, some good educational fun can be had with your child.

WRITING

My specialism is teaching kids how to write well. The mix of instruction and writing exercises that follows will give your child the opportunity to hone her linguistic intelligence, so that she becomes more technically adept, more imaginative and, ultimately, a better writer.

One way into this is for her to be taught the nuts and bolts of the language, the parts of speech. While at school I never really understood why we needed to know this technical stuff, but I've since learned that once a child has an idea about which word performs which function, then you can take a mechanistic approach to teaching her the fundamentals of good writing. 'Bung an adjective in here, put an adverb after the verb, and Bob's your uncle – and your grade's higher too.' Understanding the mechanics of a sentence helps kids to become analytical about their own writing, and gives you a means of communicating easily what they can do to improve things.

As a result of the national literacy strategy, which appears to have genuinely improved standards in primary schools, very few eleven-year-olds will leave their primary nowadays without a working knowledge of grammar. They enter secondary schools as experts in homonyms, homophones and synonyms, where they will be taught by an English teacher who thinks a preposition is when you ask someone out to dinner. It is an area we don't always do well in schools. The rudiments of it are not at all difficult, yet every year the CBI publishes a swingeing report on school leavers' lack of grammatical skills. Either the CBI are simply acting on a prejudiced kneejerk, coloured by an overestimation of their own skills at the same age, or there is a crisis in this area. It may be that, among all the formulaic and fairly pointless studies of how to interpret a photo in a magazine article, English teachers are simply forgetting to teach how the language works. I doubt this, but it is possible that it is one of those areas in which each successive teacher assumes that the job has already been done. Either that or grammar is perceived as so deeply unsexy that teachers avoid it.

Whatever the cause, to be able to make a decent fist of English grammar is absolutely vital if your child's written work is to be successful, and I make no apologies for dwelling on it so heavily in the pages that follow. Your child may not get chapter and verse on this at school, and it's also within the realms of possibility that you, too, fear the question, 'What's an adverbial start?' A little brush-up on the fundamentals might be of use to all concerned.

Even if your child is a natural at expressing herself, it is essential she grasps the rudiments of language composition if she is to attain the highest grades. For those who struggle with it, anything you can do as a parent to help them with this learning is going to pay off. So alongside an explanation for each part of speech are some ideas for simple games you can play with your child to check she has an understanding of the basics; and from there you can both move on to the stuff that is really going to pay dividends in terms of her written work.

Nouns

There are two kinds of nouns: the common noun, which is a thing word and doesn't have a capital letter unless it is used to start a sentence; and the proper noun, which is a name word and does. Banana, head and wheelbarrow are common nouns; London, Blair and Uruguay are proper.

Try this at home (or in the car)

Play this version of 'I Spy' with your child while in the kitchen or in the car, getting her to point out common and proper nouns to you as and when she sees them. 'I spy with my little eye . . . a sign, which is a common noun, for Milton Keynes, which is a proper noun.' A general rule is, if you can see it, it's a common noun (unless it's a Hoover, which is a brand name and therefore proper, or a person).

Verbs

Verbs are action words. The way I teach them can be easily transferred into the home environment. I simply ask my classes to stand up and perform the actions to the verbs I shout out.

Try this at home

If you do this at home with your child, you might want to give her the instruction, 'Run on the spot,' then go and do the shopping or make that phone call you've been meaning to make. Alternatively, you could shout the following instructions for her to act out: 'Walk on the spot. Breathe. Eat. Think. Masticate (careful with this one). Drum. Bite. Stand. Cluck. Flap. Sit. Turn. Catch. Shine. Shrink. Sing. Dance. Mow. Wash (the dishes). Clean (your bedroom). Make (your father and me a nice cup of tea). Go (to bed).'

Voilà. Bedtime negotiated with a learning experience attached. You may sit back with the fresh cup of tea that your (now sleeping) child has made you, secure in the knowledge that you are a great parent and a complete bastard all in one gorgeous educational package.

If your child is a different gender to you, there is a fun way of conjugating the verb 'to be' I learned this year from the jolly headmaster of a private school. You sit opposite each other and take turns pointing as you conjugate. The female takes her turn first, and you proceed as follows:

I am – she points at herself
You are? – the man points at her
He is – she points at him

She is – he points at her

We are – bring both arms round as if cuddling a particularly fat aunt

You are – he holds his arms wide open, indicating a load of imaginary people, including the person opposite

They are – she also indicates a load of imaginary people, over her shoulder

You can ask your child to conjugate any verb using these hand movements to show she knows how it works. Of particular use when modelling the technique to your child are the verbs 'to stink' and 'to fart'. 'I stink' (points at self), 'You stink' (points at parent), 'He stinks' (points at brother), and so on.

Adjectives

There's a really irritating advert on telly. 'This isn't just a cherry,' a sultry, pre-orgasmic female voice informs you, 'it is a ripe, glazed, handpicked, Italian Morello cherry.' 'Oh,' you think, 'how stupid of me to think it was just a cherry!' 'This isn't just a chicken,' the voice continues, breathlessly, 'it's a hand-reared, corn-fed, really good-looking, really sexy chicken . . .'

This isn't just an advert. It's a perfect example of how you can use a collection of adjectives to encourage someone to buy something at a higher price than you would pay for the same thing in another shop. They have dressed the chicken, the cherry, whatever it is, in a cloak of attractive descriptors ('ripe', 'glazed', 'corn-fed') to make you believe that, somehow, their food is so much more than just food.

Those 'descriptors' don't have to be just one word either. You can join different parts of speech (usually, though not always, with a hyphen) to make what is called a compound modifier or compound adjective, such as 'easily-forgotten', as in 'an easily-forgotten birthday'. These may not look like adjectives, but they are, and they will earn your child extra marks in written work.

Buckaroo was a game we played as children back in the seventies, but you can still buy it at Toys R Us. The aim of the game is to load items carefully on to the saddle of a grimacing plastic mule who looks as if he's just endured a particularly cold enema. If you're too heavy-handed, the bucking bronco takes umbrage and bucks off his saddle along with everything the players have loaded on to it. In my version of the game, before you take your turn, you have to describe each item you load on to the saddle with two adjectives (excluding the colour of the object), e.g. 'a sloppy, brimming bucket'. This way, your child gets good practice at using interesting describing words, and the process encourages her to be as inventive as possible. Building a good bank of adjectives will improve her written skills, and therefore her grades.

If you prefer your children to be doing something more constructive when they learn, the process can be applied to most household chores (not to mention games other than Buckaroo). You could ask your child to lay the table with you. As you lay out each implement, use two adjectives to describe each one. 'I am laying a cotton, checked tablecloth.' 'Well, I am putting down an elegant, crystalline cruet set.' Until such time as the whole table is laid.

Liberal use of adjectives will make your child's writing more vivid. However, by the time she gets past SATs exams in Year 9, it is best to be more sparing with them, as too many adjectives make writing childlike. Routinely bunging two of them before every noun will stick out like a sore thumb, and it'll destroy the rhythm of her writing. It is the choice of adjective and variety of usage that will draw the marks.

Adverbs

An adverb is an 'ly' word. It is a description of an action that you add to a verb.

With the exception of any race relations issue, I'll often ask myself the question, 'What would Big Ron Atkinson do here?' There is a wealth of information you can pick up about usage of English language from studying the utterances of Big Ron, not least in terms of his football manager's usage of the adverb. If you watch *Match of the Day*, you'll have noticed that football managers and pundits never put the 'ly' bit of the adverb on. When conjugating the past tense of the verb phrase 'to do nicely', Big Ron would say: 'I done nice, You done nice, He/She done nice, We done nice, You done nice, But the boy Rooney done magnificent.'

Correct pronunciation of adverbs is vital if you don't want your children spending their adult lives haunting touchlines in sheepskin coats, shouting at people.

Try this at home

Decide on an action – it could be brushing your hair, frying an egg or even going to the loo. Now call out a list of adverbs, asking your child to act out the action in the manner of the adverb. Your first instruction might be 'clumsily'. At which point a child miming going to the loo will slide off the imaginary toilet and crash to the floor in a fit of poor coordination. You might follow this up with the firm but gentle instruction 'sophisticatedly', at which point she will slide back on and affect a manner befitting Grace Kelly sipping a glass of champagne. (Avoid issuing the instruction 'messily' at this point.)

You could also play adverb charades by asking your child to mime adverbs she's come up with herself. You have to guess the adverb she's performing.

Another way of doing this, which for some reason works very well with teachers, is asking her to moan in the manner of an adverb. Again, call out a number of adverbs and get your child to moan, for instance, 'sadly, seriously, shrilly, silently [this one's a doozy, and is the form of moaning I prefer listening to], sleepily, slowly, smoothly, softly, successfully'. This also serves to illustrate the nuances of which the human voice is capable.

A word of caution. Not all words that end in 'ly' are adverbs – silly, ugly and smelly, for example – and not all adverbs end in 'ly'. 'Pooh silly' and 'Pooh ugly' are not instructions, they are insults. You may well be able to pooh silly, but it is not grammatically correct to do so, and as such it is not recommended by this English teacher. 'Pooh smelly' is either pidgin English or tautological, and should be avoided on both counts.

Pronouns

A pronoun goes in place of a noun. 'Man' is a noun. The pronoun you would use to replace man is 'he', unless the man is particularly unpopular that day, in which case the pronoun 'it' might be used. They're not very sexy, pronouns. And there's not a great deal to learn about them.

Conjunctions

These are the words that link two different sentences and make them into one. In schools, they are called connectives.

There are two kinds of conjunctions. The first kind work on a simple 'cause and effect' basis. They advance the sentence by showing a causal link between one clause and the next. For instance, 'Joe was thirsty [which is the cause], so [the conjunction] he bought a bottle of Tizer [the result].' The first clause doesn't have to cause the second; in some cases it might be the other way round: 'Joe bought a bottle of Tizer [which is the result], for [the conjunction] he was thirsty [the cause].' Whatever the scenario, the causal link is there. These are straight conjunctions (or connectives).

The other kind cause the sentence to kind of reverse on itself. 'Joe was thirsty [the cause], however [conjunction] he was absolutely potless and couldn't even afford a Panda Pop, let alone a whole bloody bottle of Tizer [the reversal].' We will call these counter-conjunctions (or counter-connectives). Here is a table showing a few of each variety:

Straight conjunctions	Counter-conjunctions
And	But
For	Yet
So	However
Because	Although
Since	Though
Then	Whereas
Consequently	While
Subsequently	Antithetically

Try this at home

Your child's ability to use a range of different connectives is part of the criteria for assessing writing, so it's important she understands how conjunctions work. Here's a game for teaching the variety of different conjunctions devised by an English teacher who lives in my house.

The rules are, I thought, quite simple, but I have tried this with teachers, and they have sat there looking nonplussed, so maybe it's harder than I thought. It's kind of like pass the parcel without the parcel – or, erm, the passing.

You start off by sitting in a circle and simply using the words 'connective' or 'counter-connective'. The first person might say 'connective', which means the person to her left now has a go. If she, in turn, says 'connective', then it passes to the person to her left; but if she says 'counter-connective', it passes back to the person on her right. Basically, saying 'connective' makes the direction of the game continue as it was, while 'counter-connective' makes it reverse. This is in imitation of the way the conjunctions work within a sentence: one shows a causal link that moves the sentence forward; the other makes it reverse.

It gets more complicated when the person who started the turn replaces the words 'connective' and 'counter-connective' with actual conjunctions like 'and' and 'but'. 'And' will keep things going in the same direction, 'but' will reverse it. The next time 'for' and 'yet' join opposing sides, followed by 'so' and 'however', 'because' and 'although', until such point as you are playing the game with a full range of conjunctions. You are out of the game if you either miss your turn or jump in when you shouldn't have. It is vastly more difficult than it sounds. Eventually, you have a room full of people having to use a full range of conjunctions, and having to think – quickly – about their relative functions. You have to really engage your brain to be successful in this game.

It's a really useful exercise prior to SATs, as use of a range of different connectives is one of the key criteria for assessing writing. If you've got the whole family round, make sure Gran's teeth are firmly fixed when she tries 'antithetically' on for size. It's also something that could profitably be transferred to a long car journey, or used as a cognitive warm-up before undertaking an essay.

Prepositions

Prepositions, as we know from chapter 6, are position words. It is naughty to end sentences with them.

Try this at home

You might be familiar with the parlour game Consequences. You can play this at home with at least two people, but the more the merrier. Take a piece of paper, write down the name of a man, then write 'met', fold over and swap with your neighbour. Your neighbour then writes down the name of a woman, and 'at'. Then comes a place, 'he said' and 'she replied', folding and swapping after each one, till finally someone writes 'and the consequence was'. Some strange relationships will have formed by the time you open the paper to read the final version. Just as a reminder of how it can work, here's the result of one I just did downstairs with the missus and an alarmingly articulate eight-year-old: 'Michael Portillo met Po [the Teletubby] at the top of the Eiffel Tower. He said to her, "Hello, love. I like your eyes." She replied, "Have you seen my noo noo?" And the consequence was: they decided to sleep in the library because there was a blizzard.'

You can use a bastardized version of Consequences to cement and check your child's knowledge of the parts of speech.

The formula is as follows (fold over and swap after each word):

1. An article (definite or indefinite: 'the' or 'a') followed by an adjective. An example would be 'A colossal'.
2. Another adjective. Example 'smelly'.
3. A common noun. Example 'hose'.
4. A verb (present tense). Example 'farts'.
5. An adverb. Example 'slowly'.
6. A preposition. Example 'above'.
7. Another article (definite or indefinite), followed by another adjective. Example 'the pretty'.
8. Another common noun. Example 'table'.

Unfold the paper, and you'll have, provided the parts of speech were correct, a sentence, in this case 'A colossal, smelly hose farts slowly above the pretty table.' Now, this may not be something you see very often in your day-to-day life, but it is, in the surreal world of possibility that can be created by words affixed together randomly, entirely possible.

The sentence will not work without the parts of speech being properly recognized. If you bung an adjective where you've been asked for an adverb, then all hell breaks loose with the sentence construction, e.g. 'A colossal, smelly hose farts big above the pretty table.' You can fart slowly, but you cannot fart big. To check that the sentence is grammatically correct, I ask students to act it out. If it is possible in a surreal universe, then the sentence is grammatically correct.

I make people do this stuff for a living, which is the cause of unceasing mirth to me. Until you've made a primary school head teacher in Sheffield pretend that she is 'a sickly, purple elephant living sexily under a spotty lobster' and then been paid handsomely for doing so, your life up to that point has been naught but waste and sham.

Combining parts of speech

Once kids have access to the constituent parts they can start to build the complex machinery of a decent sentence. In class, I do an exercise in which I walk across a room and ask the kids to write what they have just seen. You might expect that they'd write something like 'The stupid, scrawny teacher in a coat two sizes too big for him . . .' But no. What you get, unless they are particularly gifted or a bit of a show-off, is 'The man walks across the room.'

This is what is known in staffrooms countrywide as 'crap writing'. It is easily remedied, however. If your child has a grasp of the nuts and bolts, and can tell a noun from an adjective, a verb from an adverb, then it is a pretty quick process for her to change this bald, flat, uninspiring sentence into something that breathes and swings.

I walk across the room again, asking them to study me intently and to choose twenty different adjectives that might be used to describe my appearance. You have to be brave for this, as they will be vicious, and out of the mouths of babes come unpalatable truths. Once they have drunk in the full depths of my decayed appearance, I get them to write the adjectives in pairs in a line down the left-hand side of the page. They will generally come up with a list that starts something like this:

Aged, tired
Bloated, arthritic
Puffy, ill-kempt

Once they have done this, we move on to the noun. 'Man' was their first thought. I ask them to look at me again, and directly to the right-hand side of the adjectives write some more interesting and more original nouns. Again, they are rarely merciful.

Derelict
Toilet-cleaner
Pensioner

We move on to the verbs. There are more ways of moving across a room than walking. By way of an illustration, I might amble across the room, then skip back. They write the verbs to the right-hand side of the nouns.

Saunters
Lounges
Perambulates

Then come the adverbs.

Cleverly
Shamefully
Disconsolately

Finally, I ask them to add 'across the room' to the end of each collection of words, so that we now have three different sentences, all of which are better than 'the man walks across the room', and none of which will make the teacher feel better about himself:

The aged, tired derelict saunters cleverly across the room.
The bloated, arthritic toilet-cleaner lounges shamefully across the room.
The puffy, ill-kempt pensioner perambulates disconsolately across the room.

Using parts of speech to improve your child's writing

Your child may have a high linguistic intelligence and therefore a natural aptitude with language, but she must have some awareness of the rules of English grammar to give structure to her written language. Many kids have an excellent imaginative command of vocabulary, but little command of sentence structure or punctuation. It is not enough to use swathes of interesting language if they cannot apply the grammatical rules. It will sometimes be OK for them to break these rules . . . provided they are, first of all, able to use the language in its formal, 'correct' sense and they are making a conscious decision to break them because dispensing with the rules leads to their writing being more stylish. A case in point is grammar rule number one:

1   **Never start a sentence with a conjunction.**

If you think about the function of a conjunction (I feel a song coming on), which is to join two clauses together, then it is obvious that one can't be at the beginning of a sentence. It is the bit of filler over the join, and as such it has to be in the middle.

Or so you'd think. If you open the pages of a broadsheet newspaper nowadays you'll find that they are infected with hundreds of sentences starting with either 'and' or 'but'. You might even find a few examples in this book, for such a practice is slowly becoming fashionable, and acceptable, especially for the purposes of slamming home an additional or contrary point in an argument. Newspaper editors, journalists and publishers may be relaxed about this rule, but they are not being examined by taskmasters as harsh as the GCSE examiners. As a rule, it is better to teach children not to do it, until such time as they are scratching a fraction of their living from writing for a broadsheet. And then it is the one real perk of the job.

2 Don't put an adverb between 'to' and a verb.

This is called a split infinitive, and it will get you arrested in certain parts of Middle England. There are no doubt examples of this in the book too, but I have already been tried and acquitted of this crime in the seventies, and under the double jeopardy laws can't be tried again. So, no letters please.

To remedy a split infinitive, just bung the adverb after the verb. If your children master this easy little skill, their English teacher will cease to continually complain and start to complain continually.

3 Don't use the same pronoun twice in a sentence.

This is a more specific extension of the old 'don't use the same word twice in a sentence' rule. While it isn't strictly true that you shouldn't, your child's writing will be more stylish if she keeps an eye out for it. For instance, 'If you have a sentence with two of the same pronoun in it, you swipe the second out' is better as 'If you have a sentence with two of the same pronoun in it, swipe the second out.'

4 Don't end sentences with a preposition.

There's an old gag about this: saying 'This is the kind of grammar up with which I cannot put' instead of 'This is the kind of grammar I cannot put up with'. Technically, the former sentence is correct, but it's unwieldy and clumsy when compared to the grammatically incorrect version. So, again, your child should go with what feels best here, but bear the rule in mind. The most important point is that she is able to manipulate the sentence sufficiently well. 'She is the person with whom I came' makes her sound posh and clever, whereas 'She is the person I came with' doesn't.

5 Beware the past tense of the verb to be!

This often affects young Londoners, though there are dialect versions all over the country that also fail to conjugate this correctly. Instead of 'I was', 'you were', 'he was', etc., cockney kids often use 'was' all the way through: 'you was', 'we was', etc. They forget completely about the existence of the word 'were'. You speak how you like as far as I'm concerned, but when these speech patterns are replicated in written form they look plain wrong and get kids who speak working-class dialects punished in the exam room – which can't be right. So make sure your child knows to say 'We weren't doing anything, sir', not 'We wasn't doing anything' (or even 'We wasn't doing nothing' – see next point).

6 Avoid double negatives.

These are a no-no, though they often appear in the exercise books I mark. The statement 'We wasn't doin' nuffink, sir' should be treated with caution by any teacher: not only is it bad grammar, but, since a double negative makes a positive, it is confirmation that they must indeed have been doing somefink.

Notice, too, that they 'must have' done somefink, not 'must of'. This kind of pronunciation confusion crops up all too often in children's schoolwork. Kids often don't understand that the contraction they use for must have is 'must've', not 'must of', which in certain accents sounds remarkably similar. The same thing applies to should've, could've, would've and might've. They should also be taught by someone – please – that something, nothing, everything and anything, end in 'g'.

7 Avoid tautology.

Tautology – saying the same thing twice in successive words – is also worth knowing about and pointing out to your child so she can avoid it. It is all the rage in parts of the East End: note the number of pubs by the name the Royal Sovereign. As another example, there's no point in students writing about a 'free gift'. All gifts are, by their very nature, given free of charge, so the word 'free' here is tautological. The Department of Education should probably quit referring to 'new innovations in the curriculum' as well.

Try this at home: The Captain Kirk Test

Q. How many different errors can you spot in the well-known phrase 'To boldly go where no man has gone before'?

A. Captain Kirk was wrong in three ways:

1 'To boldly go' is a split infinitive. It should be 'to go boldly'.
2 The use of 'before' is tautological. If 'no man has gone' to these new worlds and new civilizations, then it's bloody obvious they won't have been there 'before'.
3 No 'man', Captain? What about the ladies? That Lieutenant Uhura is a funny-looking bloke . . .

Sentences

Being able to write with a variety of sentence lengths and constructions is useful for SATs tests and GCSEs in any subject. It is pretty much the definition of a stylish writer; it shows your child is aware of the rhythm of her writing, and this will come across to a reader. I have an easy way of practising this to ensure it gets into your child's head, so that they become interesting writers who score good grades in written activities.

Ask your child to pick a series of five numbers between one and five, preferably a few of the same number (for rhythm's sake – this will become clear); then to select a further five numbers between six and twenty. Mix them all up so you have a list of numbers that looks something like this: 3, 3, 2, 18, 19, 7, 1, 20, 6, 1.

Now pick a subject for a piece of writing. In this case, we'll have the moment two cars crash into each other.

Metal hits metal. Collapsing on impact. Windscreens erupting. Orange light refracts off pieces of glass throwing prism shapes on to the petrol sheen of the tarmac. Flames cover the drivers, who struggle: screaming pigs, seeking to free themselves from the inferno which is their seat. Licked by death, they cease to fight. Incinerated. These crisp, lifeless monsters: still at the same point at which the fires finally cut them free from their seatbelts. It is a barbecue for cannibals. Tasty!

Come exam time, to save your child time thinking up sentence lengths, remind her to use her (or your) mobile phone number, and write it at the top of the page. As an example, here is the phone number of someone I don't much like. Feel free to call it and leave rude messages. 07949 159658. Where there is a 'zero' in the number, suggest that she replaces it with a 'nine', and join a 'one' to its nearest neighbour (for exam purposes, one-word sentences are probably best avoided). So, for this phone number there'll be 9, 7, 9, 4, 9, 15, 9, 6, 5, 8 on the top of her page. This will ensure that her writing is rhythmic and punchy. When she runs out of digits, she can use another person's phone number.

Any decent writing benefits from a variety of sentence lengths. Giving yourself a limit on the amount of words you use forces you to be experimental with the construction of sentences. Deliberate repetition of sentence length can have a definite effect on the reader, though: the three short sentences at the start of the recent example make for a dramatic opening.

It is also vitally important that your child varies her sentence openings. I have lost count of the number of times I have set this as a target on a child's book. Have a look at a paragraph in which the same word starts every sentence – it sticks out like a sore thumb on a dog's dinner. 'I went to the shops. I bought a pint of milk. I opened the milk. I spat it out. I said to myself, "Strewth, how long has that been on the shelf?" I resolved never to enter the shop again.' Not only does the repetition of the pronoun at the front of the sentence reveal the writer to be self-obsessed, it is boring to read. The way a sentence is started affects the rhythm in much the same manner as sentence length. A little jigging about, however, and you have, 'I went to the shop, and bought a bottle of milk. Ripping the top off, I drank. "Strewth!" I said, spitting it out. "How long has that been on the shelf?" Never since that day have I entered that shop.' It's unlikely to win the Booker Prize, but it's certainly more fluid.

The fog index

While a humble correspondence clerk at Abbey National plc in the early nineties, I learned about something they called the 'fog index'. This rule of plain English suggested that thirteen words is the optimum sentence length for clear communication, twenty words is generally the maximum acceptable length, and that if you write a sentence over twenty words long it will become increasingly difficult for the reader to understand the longer it gets. The irony is not lost on me that that sentence explaining the fog index is fifty words long, and it is rather too mechanistic a way of looking at language for most adults (if not for the employees of the Abbey National correspondence section), but I think it of some use for children who are learning how to write.

Firstly, it is a reminder that you must write in sentences. Secondly, it signals that endless sentences linked with 'and' and 'then' are unlikely to get you the top grades. And the principle is sound. If I take that fifty-word sentence and reduce it to twenty words – 'The fog index tells you thirteen-word sentences are best, twenty words is the maximum, and anything over's too much' – it's certainly a bit easier to understand.

Where I draw the line is at the idea that thirteen words is the ideal sentence length for clear communication. This figure seems to have been plucked out of the air. 'Sod off' is a two-word sentence and communicates well enough for my liking. 'No' is also a clearly understandable sentence, unless you work with television people, in which case its meaning is obviously a touch more vague.

Paragraphing

Why do we use paragraphs? Some might answer that we use them to group ideas together, but this is merely an expedient to explain the real reason. The real reason we use paragraphs will only become apparent to you if you ever have cause to sit down and mark Kylie's twelve-page-long fairy story with character names taken from *EastEnders* and no paragraph breaks. It's a tough trawl marking a twelve-page-long fairy story in any case, but if Kylie hasn't indicated the point at which the poor reader might take a breather, then those twelve pages stretch out like the Sahara, with neither an oasis nor the prospect of a toilet break.

A useful exercise here is to grab a piece of white A4 paper, and draw a dot in the centre. Once you've done this, draw four further symbols in the corners (for argument's sake: a star in the top left corner, a circle in the top right, a square bottom left and a triangle bottom right). Once you have done this, take your child forcibly by the arm and make her stare at the dot in the centre. Once she's done this for long enough to make her eyes water, get her to close her eyes for ten seconds, and then reopen them. Ask her which of the symbols her eyes alighted on. If she answers anything but the star, cuff her soundly around the head and send her off to bed without supper.

The human eye, when given something to focus on, will alight immediately on the top left, then the bottom right, then the top right, and finally the bottom left. This is the reason why you shouldn't indent paragraphs: it doesn't work in harmony with the way your eyes function. If the eye immediately goes to the top left-hand corner of a piece of writing and you have indented a paragraph, upon what will it have alighted? That's right – sod all. It makes sense to me, therefore, to dispense with the indentation. I am quite strict about this. I get the odd letter in green ink from people about education issues. If the paragraphs on the letters are indented, I guarantee they will get a cursory and abrupt reply. Lay your paragraphs out without indents, however, and I will come to your house, wherever it is in the country, and tutor your children for neither money nor cups of sweet tea.

Oh yeah, and since indents are the work of the devil, get them to leave a line gap between paragraphs. Otherwise you won't be able to tell it's a paragraph break. (If I feel so strongly about it, you might well ask, why are the paragraphs in this book all indented? The answer is, because I lost the fight, and it was a bloody one, with my editor.)

When kids should paragraph is pretty simple really. Occasionally, you'll come across a child who has taken a cunning, mechanistic approach to it. She'll have simply put in a new paragraph break every five lines, and I admire her ingenuity and pluck. Examiners are hard-pressed and often ill-qualified for the job. Your child might just get away with doing this, but it's probably easier to learn how to do it properly.

In the words of Winston Churchill, 'Just as the sentence contains one idea in all its fullness, so the paragraph should embrace a distinct episode.' If you think of the pen as the camera in a film, whenever the camera cuts to a new shot – a new setting, a different character, a shift in time – you start a new paragraph to indicate this.

In non-fiction writing – a history essay, for example – you start the paragraph making some kind of point, then use the rest of it to provide details backing up your point. For instance, 'I find my friend Pete's sideburns unacceptable [main point]. He describes them as being strawberry blonde, yet to me, this phrase is always just a set of smoke and mirrors to disguise gingerness [supporting point adding more detail]. As he closes in on his forties, they become flecked – nay overrun – with grey [more detail], causing him to have them cropped so close as to be almost pointless [even more detail, justifying the original point].

'His nose, on the other hand, is fantastically beautiful, and I envy it [new paragraph with new point].'

See how the camera lingers lovingly in a long paragraph focusing on Pete's ginger sideburns, before darting off to focus on his nose?

Try this at home

Read out the following to your child and ask her to shout out 'Paragraph!' where she thinks the paragraph breaks should be:

Once upon a time, there was a little girl called Little Red Riding Hood. Now she was an obedient girl, from a strong working-class extended family. They looked after each other, the Riding Hoods. Across the woods from where Red lived with her mum, dad and little brother was Granny Riding Hood's house. Gran lived on her own, and was a bit poorly. And, as was the way in distant times when the family was a properly functional unit of social cohesion and care, the younger Riding Hoods took care of the needs of their elders. Every day Red would be given the task of bringing Granny her stewed apples, prunes and other tasteless food for the toothless. On the particular day in question Red set off through the woods, with a basket of foul-smelling foodstuffs on her arm. She skipped and ambled through the woodland with not a care in the world. What she didn't know, however, was that she had been spied by the wicked old wolf. The wolf was a sly old dog and a bit of a lazy bastard to boot. Chasing gazelles was not for him. He preferred the easy meal.

There are three natural breaks in the story:

1 The camera changes briefly to focus on Granny's house after the third sentence. It is a change of setting and should have a paragraph break.
2 'Every day' – this suggests a change of time, and is definitely a change of focus back to Little Red, and so qualifies for a paragraph break.
3 'The wolf' introduces a new character, on whom the camera would now focus.

Paragraphing rules (for fiction at least) are not set in stone, but your child should stick to these basic principles – a new setting, a different character, a shift in time – until she is a confident writer.

Punctuation

My own teaching of this subject was revolutionized by reading Lynne Truss's book, *Eats, Shoots and Leaves*. I would heartily recommend this to anyone with an interest in how to write well. Before reading it I didn't really know what to do with a semi-colon or a colon, and it was really helpful to have it spelled out exactly when it is acceptable to use a comma.

One point the book makes is that, yes, there are rules of punctuation, but there is also the matter of personal taste. (The exclamation mark, for instance, is quite beyond the pale for some people, and certainly anyone over the age of ten who uses three in a row should be forced to do some form of community service as penance.) It is useful for kids not to see punctuation as a set of constraining rules to be feared, but an opportunity to be creative with more than just the words themselves. Students who have an imaginative response to it are likely to do very well indeed.

Having said that, you've got to know the rules before you can break them, and knowledge of correct punctuation is vital for writing to communicate properly and clearly. Only this morning the lack of a full stop caused confusion in downtown Catford. A guest had arrived and was asked whether he took his coffee black. I took him to have said 'No milk and sugar' and served him up a cup of steaming hot, black, sour coffee, at which he looked disgustedly. What he had actually said was, 'No. Milk and sugar.' The punctuation makes all the difference. He may not visit again. Which suits me. I don't much like the swine in any case.

It is a more difficult intellectual process to write with half decent punctuation than it is to write interesting words, but its importance is highlighted in the criteria for both SATs and GCSE. It is experimental and creative use of a range of punctuation that will often be the difference between an A grade student in English and an A*. Let's consider briefly the use of just three of them.

Commas

There are five ways to use a comma:

1. **To separate items in lists.** This includes lists of adjectives before a noun. He was a smelly, intemperate, grumpy, badly dressed fool. Note you don't have a comma between the last adjective and the noun.
2. **Before you open direct speech.** Pete replied, 'But I like my sideburns.'
3. **Before some conjunctions.** 'I have smashingly lovely sideburns, but Pete's are a disgrace.'
4. **After an adverbial start,** i.e. when you start a sentence with an adverb, an 'ly' word: 'Unbelievably, Pete persisted with his grey and ginger sideburns long after they had outlived their usefulness.'
5. **To mark off a subordinate clause** (see chapter 2). 'Pete, despite the best advice of his friends, continued to embarrass himself and his whole extended family by sporting a hideous pair of Midge Ures.'

Semi-colons and colons

I was taught that colons and semi-colons indicated the length of the pause a reader should take. A comma is a brief respite, which is trumped by a semi-colon, which is, in turn, trumped by a colon.

According to Ms Truss, however, a semi-colon is basically shorthand for the phrase 'and another thing' (or similar). So any use of it would generally occur between the end of a sentence and an afterthought. 'Jemima is clever, industrious, polite, charming, beautiful, funny, sensitive, kind, fresh-smelling and gentle; but she needs to tidy her room more often.'

The semi-colon is also used as demarcation between two unequal clauses. The first clause above, in which Jemima's positive attributes are listed, is thirteen words long; the bit after the semi-colon, nine. This, again, is a fairly mechanistic way of looking at it, and in truth we are more concerned with the relative weight of the clauses than we are with the length of them. For students first starting to experiment with more advanced forms of punctuation, however, length of clause is a decent place to begin looking. The colon, on the other hand, demarcates two equal clauses. As with the semi-colon, the most easily understood way of looking at this is to illustrate it with two clauses of exactly the same length. 'My dad's old: he's ugly too.' The colon here is a point of balance between the two clauses, which makes it a fairly easy thing to demonstrate visually.

Another way of looking at a colon is that it shows a set-up, or a lay-up. If you imagine a tennis player throwing the ball up for a serve, or a volleyball player laying up the ball for his teammate to execute a smash (a spike, I believe they call it), then the colon shows this metaphorically. It marks the time between the linguistic equivalent of a ball leaving the hand and it being smashed. A case in point: the sentence you are reading now. The 'case in point' sets up expectation (imagine the ball arcing in the air), and 'the sentence' is the fulfilment of this expectation (the racket, or hand, connecting with the ball, smashing it).

Colons are also used to demarcate the space between an explanatory clause and a list of items used as examples of this explanation. 'There are many and varied forms of punctuation: the comma, full stop, colon and semi-colon.' Or, alternatively, 'There are many reasons Pete should get rid of the sideburns: they're an unpalatable shade, he's too old for ornate facial hair, and it'd make his mum happy.'

Similes and metaphors

Lastly, similes and metaphors are crucial aspects of any decent writing. A simile is where you compare an object or person to something else ('She entered the room like an angry weasel'). A metaphor is where you state that the object or person *is* that other thing ('She entered the room, an angry weasel').

Metaphorical language used sparingly can make a piece of writing striking and sophisticated. A metaphor is worth two similes in anybody's money, and to write a decent metaphor is to take a risk. 'Her hair is a packet of crisps' requires more of an imaginative leap than to suggest it is *like* a packet of crisps. Metaphors, like a double-piked back-somersault with two twists and a half-skank in a diving competition, have a greater degree of difficulty. As such, when properly or imaginatively achieved, they score higher marks. To change the similes to metaphors, you just take out the word 'like' (or 'as' if that is what they have used).

Try this at home

Try this metaphor-generating exercise with your son or daughter. You can enter a surreal realm where anything is possible. For argument's sake we will use the hair, mouth, eyes, nose and skin framework, and then just randomly select objects with which to construct metaphors. A book, an envelope, a tin of sweetcorn, a screwdriver and some cigarette papers are objects I can see in the room in which I am writing this (the sweetcorn is a long and convoluted story). So,

His hair is a book
His mouth is an envelope
His eyes are sweetcorn
His nose is a screwdriver
His skin is cigarette paper

Then we have to find a way to justify these nonsenses.

> His hair is a book: it is red.
> His mouth is an envelope – always open, unless it's got
> something in it.
> His eyes are sweetcorn: yellow and beady.
> His nose is a screwdriver: long and pointy.
> His skin is cigarette paper: gossamer thin and sticky
> if you lick it.

This is a great way to encourage your child to be creative with language within her written work; and the fact that it is all randomly generated gets away from her fear of getting things wrong. Throwing a few randomly generated metaphors into her writing will give your child's teachers a pleasant surprise when they are reading and marking her work. It is just such a surprise that will give the teacher reason to praise the work.

Exercises to improve writing

We're now getting into some of the subtler ways your child can start to really improve her writing. In the Original Writing element at GCSE, for example, it's essential to steer children away from the kind of story that is driven by a list of chronological events. 'We went to the shop, then we bought a bottle of milk, then the examiner gave up on us, chucked our paper in the bin, awarded us an F and went down the pub' – that sort of thing. In exams, stories where what happens is more important than how it is described produce poor writing and poor grades.

One way of avoiding this pitfall is to completely change focus and encourage your child to write in the present tense about the moment – the very moment – that something happens. It could be a flower opening, a marriage collapsing, or some profound realization or religious conversion. The constraints of focusing on a tiny moment in time will help her develop her style. She can't just go off and add another event to the story to drive her writing forward; she must sit and think, and choose her words carefully.

Put yourself in an examiner's shoes (although this is something I wouldn't normally advise: Hush Puppies are hideous). Most of what he has to read will fall into the chronological, events-driven category. I repeat, for the purposes of exams, it isn't the story that is important, it is how it is written that counts.

Observational writing

Put simply, writing decent descriptive prose requires more skill and more style than just making up stories. But what to describe? Observational writing is a useful exercise for developing these skills. Kids who love words and finding new ways to use language find this exercise really stimulating. Think of an artists' drawing class. An object is placed in the middle of the room – a bowl of fruit or an old bicycle – and they are asked to draw it. You can do the same thing with writing, with really good results.

Try this at home

Place an object on the table or on the floor and ask your child to write a description of it. It is better that this object has some history: her father's jacket will have more resonance for her than an orange (one would hope). It must be written in the present tense – 'It is lying on the floor' rather than 'It was . . .'

Initially, she may not come up with very much. 'It is a grey jacket with pinstripes . . .' Suggest she takes a metaphorical approach to it, imagining the jacket's sleeves as glacial valleys, or that the jacket is laid out like Jesus on the cross. She could personify it, guess at its history. How does it feel, lying there on the floor? Now ask her to empty the pockets and describe what she finds. What does this tell her about the person who owns, or owned, the jacket?

Then ask her to write a further present-tense section to the story about how the person who owned the jacket lost it. Writing in the present tense about past events employs a narrative device called 'present tense flashback'. Provided her punctuation and choice of language are both accurate and imaginative, it will hit the criteria for an A* in the Original Writing element of GCSE English Language.

Let me take the art student analogy a little further. You'll recall they also do what they call 'life drawing', in which a naked fat bloke sits there embarrassed, worried about how small his willy is, while a group of art students cast his obesity in charcoal hues. Just such a technique is useful for developing your child's ability to create characters in her writing.

A character is two things: what someone looks like, and what they do. Sadly, our imaginations are sometimes not enough on their own, but acute observation of real life can be used to provide more finely observed detail. What a character looks like is easy. Your child can look closely at someone and describe him or her. At home she can describe you; in class she can describe her classmates; and, crucially, in an exam room it would be a fantastic piece of opportunism to use what is around her, and paint a literary picture of the poor sod in the squeaky shoes walking up and down the lines slurping cold coffee and going, 'Shush!' Combine this with the earlier exercise on sentence length in an exam room, and an exceptional grade is a cast-iron certainty.

So, the phone number 07775 123456 would lead to 97775 123456, which would lead to 9, 7, 7, 7, 5, 12, 3, 4, 5, 6. Which, combined with the observation of someone's face, leads to the production of a piece of writing like this:

> One slim shoulder is held slightly below the other. Her hair a bun of loose curls. She wears a smile of enigmatic sincerity. Two silver rings dangle from her ears. She leans forward and speaks. Her brows arch in slight confusion as she chats to the boy. Small pixie-like ears. A nose noble, proud. And two slender, intelligent eyebrows. They live above darting green pools.

This description is of an everyday domestic event: Mrs Beadle cleaning the baby's high chair. It doesn't do her justice. Taken out of the context in which it is written, however, we can see the beginnings of a character. This description could be of a princess, a Roman empress, or a female faun in *The Lion, the Witch and the Wardrobe*. It could also be the beginning of a description of a bag lady, a bank teller or a prostitute (she'll be livid when she reads this). In whichever fictional scenario it was planted, it'd get reasonable grades. Because the description is drawn from real life, there is a level of detail you would be unlikely to get just from using your imagination.

Automatic writing

This is a technique used by those teachers of creative writing who clog up adult education courses in night schools across the country.

'What are we doing this evening, miss?'

'I thought we'd do some more automatic writing.'

'Oh, that's a surprise, miss. Didn't we do automatic writing last week, and the week before that?'

Its validity as a teaching tool, however, was underlined to me when I went on a course run by the poet Simon Armitage. If you don't know who Simon Armitage is, I'll give you some homework to find out. He's a down-to-earth, earring-clad, northern, poetic genius. If you think you don't like poetry, I would advise you to read some of his gear. The fact that the first thing Simon Armitage made a bunch of corduroy-clad teachers do on the course was automatic writing suggests to me that it is of some worth after all.

Basically, you just write whatever – and I mean whatever – comes into your head. It's useful to have a time limit as this breeds a sense of urgency. A typical first try at this might read something like this: 'What am I thinking? Nothing. This teacher is stupid asking me to do stupid things like this. I don't have any thoughts. Nothing. Why am I doing this? Is he mental?'

This is all very well and good in terms of helping your child express the gaping spiritual chasm in her pitiful materialistic life, but a child who has come up with such a response to the request that she write whatever comes into her head has not fulfilled the task properly. She has organized her thoughts into cohesive sentences, for a start, and this is not what she was asked to do. Thought patterns operate in an infinitely more random, more interesting way. Here is an example of some work I've kept from Peter, an ex-student:

Splurge. Thinking and pinking what is this happen fine numbers and toolies filching and cobblers is my middle name is there a path for arsenic squibble squibble and two monkeys dancing on a cake and tank forth two men there is no tanks and football when there isn't any fine fire pathways and there is no fear fighting and dunking with a dairylea dunker this is in what is in my mind poor me.

Either Peter is going to need some fairly serious therapy at some point, or this piece is actually a reasonable representation of the chaos that is every human's thoughts before order is forced upon them. Without the stricture of organization, thoughts can roam free and the most surreal connections can arise. Automatic writing is a way of tapping into that point just before you fall asleep when your thoughts turn to jelly, and from which a dream state can emerge. What comes out of this can be useful in terms of generating new ideas, titles or images.

Armitage refers to the notion of a 'neon phrase'. All his poetry seems to feature a couple of phrases that stand out, pulsing with profundity, from the rest of the words; Technicolor on monochrome. If your child is struggling to get anywhere near coming up with ideas of images for a story, then automatic writing can operate as a laxative for the brain, flushing out some of the rubbish and presenting it in a form from which you can extract images that may be of use to start off a bigger idea.

It is also of use in fighting against children's propensity towards self-censorship. Many children's writing is affected by the fear of getting it wrong. Such fear can be paralysing. It can stop them from making any mark on the page. Automatic writing is not only a quick guarantee that words will be etched on paper, it also gives permission – to experiment, to break with stultifying rules, to be brilliant or rubbish, or both at the same time. It is vital in education that children learn to embrace failure, as by failing we learn. There's a fantastic quote from the writer Samuel Beckett on this subject, which I've used from time to time in an attempt to instil the joy of failure in children I teach: 'Tried? Failed? Try again. Fail again. Fail better.'

Essays (structure and layout)

Everyone has his own opinion on how essays should be laid out. It always struck me as a bit daft that there has never been a standard policy on this, so each school ends up submitting coursework essays laid out in a thousand different ways.

One thing you will find in common is the idea of 'point-evidence-explanation', or 'PEE' for short. Deeply and tragically unfunny teachers will often instruct their children to make sure they do a 'PEE' in the exam room. It wasn't funny when some quarter-witted lame brain first coined it, and it hasn't been made any funnier by the countless thousands of repetitions to the same bored ears in classrooms across the country. My detestation for the gag has caused me to favour calling it 'idea-quote-comment'. It doesn't carry any reference to urine, but IQC does much the same practical job as a PEE.

The idea of it is that if you are writing an essay in English, there is not much point in coming up with an unsubstantiated idea. The idea that the nasty character Iago from Shakespeare's *Othello* is gay is interesting, but without any back-up it's going to get *nul points*. Any idea that a child might have about a book, a character or event must be backed up with a reference from the text, usually in the form of a quote lifted directly from its page.

'Iago is gay because, in attempting to convince Othello of Desdemona's infidelity, he says, "I lay with Cassio lately."'

Bringing in this quote (or as the PEE acronym would have it, this evidence) goes some way towards proving the point made, but not far enough. This alone will be enough to get your child a D grade at GCSE, maybe even a low C; but the big fat grades are saved for those who comment on exactly how the quote proves the idea, or who explain how the evidence backs up the point.

'As soldiers, Iago and Cassio may have had to sleep in a barracks, but Iago's testimony suggests that they were actually sleeping in the same bed. They are two of the highest-ranked officers in the Venetian army, and as such would have been the very last to be made to share a bed by circumstance. This suggests that it was of their own volition, and that they will have volunteered long before any of the lower ranks were able to suggest that they would share a bed.'

In terms of the way this is laid out, I advise that students leave a full line gap either side of any quote. This can be quite difficult for them to understand initially. I even go so far as to draw an island, and get them to explain why quotes are an island. (Because there is a sea of space around them.) Here is what it all should look like:

Iago is gay because, in attempting to convince Othello of Desdemona's infidelity, he says,

I lay with Cassio lately.

As soldiers, Iago and Cassio may have had to sleep in a barracks . . . And so on. A full comment explaining, at length, how the quote proves the idea is where all the big marks are kept. There is no point your child just writing any idea that comes into her head and leaving it unjustified. You get an F or a G for just an idea, no matter how good it is. The real marks are in finding an appropriate quote, and particularly in explaining why it's appropriate.

All teachers have a bias towards their own subjects. All have their beauties and brilliances, but I'd wager they would struggle to come up with an argument against the statement that being able to read and write well are the most important technical skills children learn at school. I'm an English teacher, so most of the exercises I give are naturally focused on learning facts and techniques associated with the study of English Language and Literature, but you can easily take the 'Try this at home' ideas in this book and, with a little thought, adapt them to any subject. If you go through the exercises in this chapter with your child, by the end of the process she will be better at writing than when you started. I have used all these techniques in the classroom, and they've produced some startling results.

Eight years ago, two very small Lithuanian girls, Roberta and Siggy, found themselves dumped, blinking like fauns in the harsh light of a Monday morning, in a classroom in East London. One could speak English, one couldn't. Both were jewels. Over the years, I used many of the techniques in this chapter with the girls and watched them grow into fantastically talented and original human beings. Siggy, the one who couldn't speak any English when we met, recently sent me one of her poems:

A soul I am, composed of silent language,
Silent form, red blood, as warm as breath
Of thy face, and tears; almost drown thee.
For every word unspoken, I
Pass my time in darkening despair.
Hide my name, un-name my breath
And speak of air, in which I do not live
Then bring forth lies, deliver'd from thy sweetest lips
That speak from where the hell in heart begins
   and silent lies
      do not deserve
        a name;
           and if my name is gentle;
           they violently decay!

Which, I think, speaks for itself.

I cannot take credit for Siggy's brilliance. It was innate. However, flowers that receive no encouragement might forget they are flowers and become something duller. I am very proud that an ex-student of mine can write with such skill and passion, and practising the techniques in this chapter may well put your own child on to the path of writing as well as this.

Above all, you should encourage your child to read for pleasure, and involve yourself in what she reads. A recently released study of academic attainment in working-class areas revealed that one of the key indicators of potential academic failure is having the *Sun* newspaper in the house as the sole form of literature. This might sound snobbish: it's a very specific and skilled technique you need to write for the *Sun*. Still, what is certain is the more books you have in the house, the more likely it is that your child will be successful at school. Fiction is better than non-fiction, particularly for boys, as it develops empathy in a way the *Guinness Book of World Records* won't; and having a parent who conspicuously enjoys reading is vital too. So, next time you are luxuriating on the sofa reading that unputdownable novel, and the children call asking you to service their inexhaustible plethora of needs, tell them you are already doing something for them.

9
Putting It All Together

Now you have access to all these new techniques with which you can involve yourself in your children's education: you may have an idea of their predominant intelligences, or how to tap into their preferred learning styles, and you'll be able to tailor the help you give them to their individual needs. You'll know all about the importance of visual stimuli and body-based activities, and once you've read and digested the remaining few chapters of this book, you'll also know how to make formative assessments of their work, and you'll have an understanding of how this should feed into what they learn next. The question now is, what do you do with all this new stuff? How do you put it all together so that you help your child achieve all he can?

A lot of research has been done into how kids best learn in terms of the amount of time they spend studying. The two elements of this that strike me as important are related to concentration and how the ways in which they are taught affect their retention of information.

Some research suggests that in any school lesson children will remember the first ten minutes and the last ten minutes of what they've done. By this measure, you wonder why on earth teachers bother with the middle bit. Most individual lessons in schools are between forty-five minutes and an hour long. If kids remember only the first and last ten minutes, that seems an obvious argument for having twenty-minute lessons. But this would mean secondary schools being in a near permanent state of lesson changeover, which would be complete chaos.

However, when children are studying at home there's not a lot of travelling involved, and, unless you are very rich, you probably don't have as many corridors in your home as you'd find in your average comprehensive. There's little reason, therefore, to extend periods of study beyond the time they are useful. Long hours spent sweating over a textbook don't necessarily induce any learning at all. There's a lot of sitting gazing at the textbook that is simply going through the motions, making the shape of someone studying without actually getting the substance.

Daniel Goleman talks about an ideal condition for learning, the 'flow' state. This is the temporary emotional state that all athletes, performers, artists and plumbers seek: to be totally on top of their game to the point where their absorption in the work in hand becomes total and they lose consciousness of anything external to that work. It is what athletes call 'being in the zone'. This wilful, temporary loss of consciousness of the self is vital to performers, and can be equally important for a child when he is studying. In *Emotional Intelligence*, Goleman describes 'flow' as 'being the state in which people become utterly absorbed in what they are doing, paying undivided attention to the task, their awareness merged with their actions'.

The trouble with such a state is, first of all, how to get into it, and secondly, the fact that it is temporary. Both are solved by taking a fairly liberal approach to studying. It's better to do it when you are in the mood. Trying to force yourself into the flow state can be counter-productive. It may be that there are certain conditions which are conducive to good study: your child might need music as a stimulus, or a reward to make studying more palatable. Alternatively, he might prefer bright light and total hush (in which case tell him to go and live somewhere else). Any of these preferences should be indulged if it heightens the possibility of him locating the 'flow zone'.

Encourage him to take frequent breaks, too, which tackles the issue of the state's temporariness. If the first and last ten minutes of any learning experience are the ones that stick, it makes sense for your child to study in short, sharp bursts. This way he can locate the flow state in which he performs most effectively and take a break when this wanes. Sometimes the best way of breaking a big rock is not by smashing it all in one go, but by chipping away at it. Your child should come back to work when his mind has been refreshed by that break.

If your child is revising and you want to help him do so effectively, you can call the breaks. Don't let him just sit there in front of the computer logging on to MySpace when he should be working: he will get lost in it and forget he should be studying. Prepare a drink or snack for him every twenty-five minutes or so, and get him to come completely away from the work. This doesn't mean he should sit in front of the telly watching whole episodes of *Casualty*. The point of a break is that after it you can restart with your brain refreshed by it. And to restart refreshed, you've got to restart.

Generally speaking, the amount of homework your child will be expected to do will increase as he travels through the year groups. Some primaries still do not set any homework at all, but this is changing as it is recognized that early parental involvement in a child's schoolwork is a key indicator of academic success; and setting homework at an early age is a pretty sure way of getting this habit ingrained before children become uncooperative. By the time they get to secondary, there is an expectation that each subject teacher will set homework at least once a week, maybe twice in the case of maths, English and science. Each piece of homework will take in the region of half an hour. This is ideal in terms of your children being able to break up their work into manageable chunks. By the time they are thirteen, in Year 9, the expectation is that they complete in the region of two hours' homework a night, building up to two and a half or three hours by the time they are taking their GCSEs. I've always felt that this is a bit much, and that kids should have time to play, relax and watch telly; but because of league tables, schools can get very anxious about the results their pupils attain. Since regular homework, completed seriously, is supposedly one of the prime means of improving results, schools will be very eager that their students do a lot of it (even though their concern with this is somewhat at odds with another of the main tasks of education, which is to produce rounded, happy, functional human beings).

Another piece of research on the effectiveness of various types of learning is, I think, fascinating for teachers: apparently, people remember only 10 per cent of what they read and 20 per cent of what they hear. If they see it, however, the figure increases to 30 per cent, and it goes all the way up to 50 per cent if they see and hear something at the same time.

Lecturing is said to be the single least effective means of learning. You can retain a person's attention for only about four minutes when you are lecturing before they drift off. Fantastically skilled lecturers can extend this to seven, but however good they are, their students will still retain only a small percentage of the information given. This is one of the reasons ceaseless lectures about kids' behaviour never seem to work. While you are launching into another impassioned rant about how he made you feel when he said, 'No, I won't pick that up. You're the household slave. You do it,' in his head your child is playing volleyball with someone attractive on a Spanish beach.

If being lectured is at the bottom of the pyramid in terms of retaining a child's interest and them holding on to the information, then at the top, somewhat surprisingly, is teaching. Teaching someone else something is the most effective way of ensuring the information stays with you. There's obviously potential to apply this fact at home. When your child has finished studying something, asking him to give you a five-minute lesson on what he has learned will lodge it indelibly in his cranium, like the setting lotion that ensures the blue rinse doesn't run embarrassingly down Grandma's neck the moment the clouds break.

During this process, it is fairly important that you don't leave stuff unclarified. Ask lots of what might seem to him (or even to you) wilfully 'stupid' questions. Asking your child to elaborate on what he is saying will cause the cognitive gears to whirr, trapping the information, in sentence form, in the language he has employed to express it. He might get uppity and think you're a bit daft, but if it saves him from flipping burgers, it's worth setting yourself up as an easy target for a while.

STRUCTURING THE LEARNING

The government recommends that teachers teach what is called a four-part lesson, which has the following elements: starter, guided, independent and plenary. The idea is that the 'starter' activity performs what is called in teaching circles 'engaging cognition'. In other words, it wakes the brain up so that it is in an enlivened state, receptive to new information. The 'guided' bit is where the teacher teaches something. Students then apply this in some 'independent' study until the point when the teacher does a recap, or 'plenary', at the end, to set the knowledge in their heads.

This lesson planning device is doubtless the result of years of the world's greatest educational brains working on the ideal learning experience, so I shan't dismiss it out of hand just yet. What is interesting about it is that the structure can be transferred to any learning you plan to do with your own children.

In a single lesson in schools, the starter, or warm-up, would take ten minutes. You would guide their learning for a further ten, then leave them to some independent educational activity for the next thirty minutes before asking them to do a ten-minute recap at the end. This is pleasingly simple, and it seems a good idea, until you remember that thirty minutes is a long time for some children to concentrate on one thing, and that each child will have his own individual needs. What it does do – and I would hope this concept has sunk in by now – is underline the fact that any learning your child undertakes should not rely on just one technique. If your child is to optimize his ability to acquire and retain information, and you are to guide him properly in doing so, there is not much point in just tapping your finger on a book and saying, 'Read that for an hour.' He'll learn next to nothing.

Starter

A lesson starter is there to get kids' brains limbered up for the task in hand. It can be as simple as a spelling test orientated around the key words and terms of the subject they are about to study. Still, since the main purpose of this is to get the neurons firing and to engage cognition, there is no reason why it has to be subject-related, or even specifically educational. I have found that getting children to transcribe the lyrics to songs is great for getting the brain into the right state for learning. A ten-minute game of Scrabble, or even Hangman (on a word specific to the subject they are about to study), would do much the same job.

It can also be a good time to link up with previous learning. Setting a small test on something they learned last week forces the brain to work at extracting the information, making it go through the recall process that embeds learning. What we use soon after doing it we remember for ever. What we don't use soon after doing it is lost for good.

Guided

Once your child has completed a starter to fire up the brain, you must tell him what he is going to learn. In schools, this process is called 'setting objectives'. All teachers write these on the whiteboard, underneath a great big sign in neon capitals that says LESSON OBJECTIVES. I'm no great fan of importing this technical teacher language into the classroom. What is the point of using the jargon 'objective' with a bunch of schoolkids? 'What is your objective?' – sounds like *Star Trek*. 'My objective is a five-year mission to discover new worlds and new civilizations.'

Kids are meant to be able to tell OFSTED inspectors what the lesson objective is. I once overheard a conversation between one of my pupils and an OFSTED inspector, which went:

'What's the lesson objective, young man?'

'It's the thing the teacher has to put on the board, that we have to copy down because he can't be bothered to do a proper starter activity.'

'No, but what is an objective?'

'I told you, it's the thing . . . the teacher . . . puts on the board. Strewth. Where did they get you from?'

'What are you learning today?' is another question entirely and is likely to achieve a more satisfying response: 'Oh, we're learning about plate tectonics and ox-bow lakes and the symbolic significance of the lighthouse in Virginia Woolf and the caves in Forster's *Passage to India*. But I can see you've got somewhere else to go.'

All talk of objectives aside, you can start by discussing with your child what he thinks he needs to learn. Looking at a teacher's comments in his book is the ideal way of finding out what this is, but there is a very good chance that your child already knows exactly where he falls down in a particular subject, and will be able to volunteer this information with the merest of shoves in the right direction.

Look at the last piece of work in that subject area with him and see if you can identify together what it is he needs to learn. Once you have done this, ask him to state in words what he needs to learn, and to write it down somewhere. This simple technique engages what educationalists call 'meta-cognition' – thinking about the learning process, and being aware of and explicit about the fact that he is learning something. It gives him an objective sense of purpose about the work, and about the fact that he is involved in a process, a voyage if you will, for which there is a definable end point: the acquisition of and secure grasp of a specific piece of knowledge. You might have identified that by the end of the session he will be able to apply Shakespeare's use of iambic pentameter to crack complex algebraic calculations, or it might be the ability to clean the sink after brushing his teeth. However simple or seemingly complex the knowledge he is to acquire, it helps if it is identified explicitly. That way your child can ask himself a simple question at the end of it. Did I learn what I set out to learn?

Once you have established what he is going to learn, you can move on to guiding him towards it.

In schools, this is the point where the teacher stands up at the front of the class and, often with the aid of an interactive whiteboard nowadays, actively teaches something. Frankly, you'd look utterly ridiculous standing in the front room brandishing a set of multi-coloured markers in front of your poor child, making wild gesticulations as you talk animatedly about geomorphology. Besides, interactive whiteboards are bulky, expensive, difficult to install and don't double very well as *objets d'art*.

However, you wouldn't look ridiculous demonstrating something to him. To take my example, I can recall from O level physics that latent heat is the amount of heat a material needs to undergo what is termed a 'change of state' (from ice to water, from water to steam, etc.). A parent who shows this to her child by going into the kitchen, grabbing a piece of ice from the freezer and timing it as she first melts it then brings it to the boil is a parent whose child is likely to be enthralled by, and thereafter fully in possession of, this new piece of knowledge.

I have always found that a good way into actually teaching kids something is to focus on the new language, or key words, they need to learn. Key words are all the rage in schools. For me, bringing new language to the pupils' knowledge, thereby enriching their vocabulary, their ability to express themselves and, consequently, their experience of life, is one of the fundamentals of teaching. A warning here, though: key words should be new vocabulary. 'Bucket', for instance, is not a key word. I have lost count of the numbers of science teachers I have seen with words like 'bucket' on their key-word boards. The idea behind defining items of vocabulary a child will learn in a lesson is that it should be new, high-order and technical. Eleven-year-olds do not need to be told what a bucket is. They already know. Lou, my youngest son, knows what a bucket is. He can pronounce the word with a beautiful cockney twang, and is fully aware, at the age of one and a half, that you can put it on your head, or wee in it before tipping it out on to the carpet (if you really want to show Mummy what a clever boy you are).

By identifying three or four new words related to a subject and then defining these for your children in an interesting and practical way, you are using a tried and tested method of equipping them with new knowledge and giving that knowledge a name.

It might be that during the guided bit, where you acquire knowledge together, you use the internet to access that information. It is a fantastic research tool, the internet, the biggest and most detailed encyclopedia in the world. Be wary, though, of your child just cutting and pasting large chunks from it, and handing it in as his own work. Kids learn nothing whatsoever this way, and it is an insult to their teachers' intelligence to imagine they won't notice. This applies equally if you do their coursework for them. Some teachers are quite clever. If a child who is struggling in class with the concept of where to place a comma hands in a piece of work with the analysis and language of an MA student, the teacher is going to notice.

I've had the brightest A* students trying to get away with this. We've sat down and had a chat during which I've pointed out that they are brilliant anyway, so why would I want to read the work of some scientist? It's the fantastic freshness and originality of the thoughts of young people that teachers entered the profession to commune with, not those of some crusty academic. After we've had our little chat, we take the piece of coursework copied from someone else and chuck it in the bin. Some schools may take a less liberal approach, though, so be wary. Handing in work copied from the internet might result in a permanent exclusion in some environments. Tory MP Boris Johnson has admitted (in a column in the *Guardian*) to having cheated himself at some point, and his thoughts on it are worth repeating here: 'Twenty-five years ago I did once cheat. I took away from that experience three sensations: that it was laborious, that it was pointless, and also that it was somehow personally dispiriting. I had done it because I wanted to dazzle and I was left with a sense of shame, especially when the librarian dobbed us in.'

If your child is going to use information from the internet, he must reconstruct it. The best way to do this is to print out several source materials, read them and take notes; then throw the source material in the bin and take a break. After the break, your child should write down what he remembers in his own words, with no further reference to the source materials. This will ensure that the research he has done is valid.

Independent

This is where your child works on some form of exercise related to what you have demonstrated to (or discovered with) them. This is the point at which teachers will distribute loads of worksheets, and students will sit and do them quietly (or so the teacher hopes). At home, this is where your child sits on his own and does the homework that has been set for him.

What you learn independently is supposedly of more value than something someone teaches you. Maybe because it involves activity on the part of the learner it is more effective. More likely it trains children in the skills of independent, self-starting study that they will need at university. Or even more likely, standing in front of a class teaching is much more strenuous than sitting watching pupils fill in endless worksheets, and teachers are always looking for an excuse to put their feet up. This might explain the predominance of the extended independent activity, or it might be that a really extended piece of work allows children to locate their flow state and gives them sufficient time to burrow their way into it.

At this point, as a parent it is better if you absent yourself. Even the most fantastic typist goes to pieces when the boss is looking over her shoulder, and so it is for your child. It is OK to be in another room, available to answer the odd question, but hovering around looking over his shoulder every five minutes is going to be seriously counter-productive. As is doing the work for him. It is *not* your homework. Your time of sitting in drafty exam rooms is over. Your child will not learn anything if you do it for him.

Generally speaking, an extended writing exercise is the most useful way of consolidating the stuff he has learned while being guided. Not only does it allow children to develop imaginative responses to what they have been taught, but practice at writing is the best way to improve it. The task set can be as imaginative as you like. 'Write a humorous story about how the first scientist to discover the existence of latent heat did so.' It could be presented in the form of stage dialogue, or as a diary or journal. It could be in poetic form, in first or third person, in past, present or future tense. The only limit when it comes to setting independent tasks for students to investigate further the knowledge they've acquired is the imagination of the person setting it.

If you feel your child isn't 'getting' it, you could try setting extra tasks. These could be visual, kinetic, mathematical or musical; you could go so far as to ask him to devise a dance illustrating latent heat, or to design a model that shows how it works using a cardboard box. That's the fantastic thing about teaching (other than the pure, unadulterated joy of working with children, and seeing them develop): it operates in the landscape of the imagination, and the more outrageously imaginative, or even silly, the task you set them, the greater the likelihood they will remember what they have been taught.

Of course, you could always just download a worksheet from the internet with a load of dry questions. However, if you are sufficiently interested in your child's education not only to have bought this book, but to have got as far as this chapter, then it's likely you are going to be sufficiently interested to ensure that whatever involvement you have in his schooling nourishes his body, mind and sense of joy.

Plenary: the recap

A couple of years ago, I wrote an article on plenaries for a teaching journal for which I was paid the equivalent of the minimum wage. While I was working on it, my wife asked me what I was doing.

'I'm writing an article about plenaries for the equivalent of the minimum wage,' I replied.

'What in God's name is a bloody plenary?' exclaimed Mrs Beadle, thinking it to be the ultimate in pointless educational jargon. After I'd patiently explained that she was right, it is the ultimate in pointless educational jargon, but it is also the bit teachers do in the last ten minutes of a lesson, recapping so that things stick in students' heads, she said, 'Oh. The varnish that seals the lesson.'

I thought that summed it up pretty well.

Varnish takes a while to set, though. An effective plenary will take a full ten minutes. Many teachers don't bother with plenaries (unless they have an OFSTED observer sitting at the back of the class, ticking boxes). They are often completely knackered by that point of the lesson, and it can be tempting to let the students get on with their quiet, independent work until the bell rings, as this requires far less energy than getting them to down tools and launch into a further activity. When they can be bothered, the plenary will often be in the shape of simply asking the students what they have learned today. This can easily backfire, as the obvious response to this is, 'Nothing. You never teach us anything. And you never mark our books. Or set us homework. And you've worn the same suit three days running now.'

Quite simply, there is not much point in teaching fantastic lessons if the information, unvarnished, is washed away at the end of the day. The theory behind the plenary states that using that part of the brain that retrieves information actually causes it to embed in our memories. It doesn't matter if the child can't extract the information without help; it is the process of trying to do it which is important. Having given his brain the workout of attempting to get the information for you, it will be in an ideal state to retain it. At home, a way of ensuring that your child retains any information he has acquired is to round off with an interesting bit of summing-up.

David Keeling, the educationalist I quoted in the introduction, came up with one plenary technique which I have stolen, without his permission, and use often. Ask your child to think of a number between one and twenty, then to write a sentence with exactly that number of words which sums up what he has learned. This is both fun and challenging.

However, it doesn't take the full ten minutes, and there are several other approaches that pay equally high dividends. You could ask your child to draw a picture or mind map (see chapter 5) that sums up the learning, and get him to talk you through it when it is done. The favoured method, though, considering that the best means of retaining information is to teach it to someone else, is to give your child five minutes to plan a mini lesson on what he has learned which he will then deliver either to you, a partner or a sibling in the final five minutes. Think of some questions to ask him as he delivers this mini lesson. This will feed his feeling of being on top of the subject, and he'll enjoy the opportunity of patronizing you at the same time as cementing the knowledge acquired.

OTHER WAYS OF PLANNING

The four-part lesson is felt by many teachers to be restrictive, and I would see it only as a basis from which to jump off and do something far more interesting. Again, the only real restriction to how you structure your children's learning is the height of your combined imaginations.

Within reason, the more activities there are in a lesson the better that lesson is. So I actually disagree quite vehemently with the government when it tells teachers that they must all follow the same four-part lesson structure. It is beneath us. A good teacher creates infinitely more exciting learning experiences, structured in infinitely more ornate and complex ways. To bind teachers to just a four-part lesson when they are capable of producing something far better seems daft.

Teaching isn't rocket science. The intellectual aspects of it can be mastered by anyone with a will to do so. You don't have to go to college for four years to learn the skills, either. They can reasonably be picked up over the space of reading a book.

Where a teacher has skills a parent might lack is in standing in front of a class of thirty kids and managing the relationships and the discipline. This is a special, complex competency acquired through years of doing it (if you manage to last that long without having had a complete nervous breakdown and running home to your mum in floods of tears, never to return). You should always respect your child's teachers for this. Having said that, though, there is no reason whatsoever why you can't engage with your child's education, understand more or less all of the principles behind the way he is being educated, and help him to attain not only the results of which he is capable, but more importantly, a lifelong sense that learning things is fun.

A wise man once said that the central tragedy of human existence is that 'Every man is born a genius and dies a fool.' At the beginning of our lives we are all fantastic, creative geniuses. The pressures of growing into adulthood can divest us of these abilities. I read a study recently that in the region of 98 per cent of children who enter reception class hit a specific measure by which they might reasonably be termed creative geniuses. By the time they leave school this quotient has evaporated in all but 2 per cent of them. Why this happens is worthy of some serious study. Whether it is a result of the pressures for conformity in school, or of learning at an early age that there is a right answer and a right way of doing things (there isn't), or whether it is simply a case that much of what goes on in schools bores the imagination out of children, it is little short of tragic. Involving yourself in your children's education, laughing with them and helping them to equate the discovery of knowledge with laughter, is, aside from showing them how to give and receive love, the greatest gift you will ever give to them.

⑩
Key Stages,
Tests and Marking

Key Stages and tests

For the uninitiated, here's a brief explanation. The British education system is separated into four (or five if you include A levels) stages, each of which is described as 'key', though some are more key than others. Your child sits SATs (Standard Assessment Tests) at Key Stages 2 and 3. These were established relatively recently and, in the case of the Key Stage 3 SATs, they are controversial among teachers, many of whom think the testing burden on children is absurd.

This prioritization of everything can be confusing for kids (not to mention parents). I've sat in September assemblies listening to the Head of Year's annual speech, in which he imparts the same message every year: 'This . . . is . . . the . . . most . . . important . . . year . . . of . . . your . . . life.' And I've overheard the whispered conversations:

'Oh. I thought last year was the most important year in our lives.'

'No. It's this year.'

'What about next year?'

'That'll be the most important year of our lives as well.'

'Shit. They're lying to us. Why are the teachers lying to us? The sky is falling in.'

In truth, some years are more important than others, and the consequences of failure can range from negligible to apocalyptic.

Key Stage	Ages	Year group	You knew it as	Exams at end of Key Stage	Consequences of stuffing them up
1	5–7	1, 2	Infant school	Teacher-assessed exams covering reading, writing and maths	There will be no lasting damage. These tests are designed to see how your child is progressing against expected standards of attainment, and to check there are no serious problems.
2	7–11	3, 4, 5, 6	Primary school	KS2 SATs in English, maths and science	No real damage, unless you are going for a selective version of secondary education. In which case, these exams are vital: your child's results will affect how these schools see her.

There are key points when things tend to go awry. The transition from primary to secondary can be enormously taxing emotionally for some kids. They may have been at their primary for up to seven years. It will have been a place where they knew everyone and in which they had only one classroom teacher who taught

Key Stage	Ages	Year group	You knew it as	Exams at end of Key Stage	Consequences of stuffing them up
3	11–14	7, 8, 9	First, second and third years of secondary school	KS3 SATs	If your child's school sets by ability in Key Stage 4, your child may find herself in one of the weaker sets, and *may* be allocated a weaker teacher.
4	14–16	10, 11	Fourth and fifth years of secondary school	GCSEs or GNVQs	Unless your child achieves five A*–C passes it is unlikely she will be able to study for A levels. Universities also require that you achieve five A*–Cs.
5	16–18	12, 13		A levels or vocational qualifications	Your child won't get on to the course, or into the university, of her choice.

*see p.237

them everything; they will now have different teachers for each subject. Physically, they must also go from being the biggest in a school to being the smallest. If you put yourselves in their shoes, you can see how that might do their heads in.

Progress in Key Stage 3 can be worryingly slow. With exams driving everything, head teachers tend to put the following weighting on year groups in terms of resources: the most important are Years 9 and 11 (exam years for both), Year 10 (GCSE coursework) and Year 7 (induction); not much happens in Year 8, so it's seen as the least important. This means that kids in Year 8 can lose their way completely. Be specifically aware of your child's performance in this year. It can be the year when she makes the decision whether she is for or against education, and the fact that it is coincidentally the year in which she is lowest down the pecking order of priority means that irretrievable disasters can happen almost unnoticed.

Marking

If your child's book remains unmarked by her teacher, then the key means through which her work, and specifically her writing, will be improved is lost. A good teacher will provide positive, detailed and helpful feedback on every piece of written work your child hands in.

Two kinds of assessment are used in schools, summative and formative.

Summative Assessment

This is easy enough to understand. The teacher sets a test; the child does the test; the teacher marks it, and puts a number in a mark book (or, nowadays, on a spreadsheet). Summative assessment tells both your child and you, the parent, where she is in a subject. A levels, GCSEs and SATs exams are merely the most obvious examples of summative assessment. They sum up and record your child's achievement in a particular subject and place her on a scale of achievement for her age.

The levels you find recorded on your child's school report up to the end of Year 9 are called National Curriculum Attainment Levels (NCAT Levels for short), and they are standardized nationally. A Level 4 student in Haringey should therefore be producing the same standard of work as a Level 4 student in Hull. The levelling is complex and can be vaporous, working on what is called a 'best fit' basis. So, if elements of your child's writing would qualify her for a Level 5 but the majority of her work is at Level 4, she will be judged as being at the lower level.

Over the last couple of years sub-levels have been added, and you will now find a letter after the number. These go from 'a', the highest, down to 'c', and give you a more exact idea of your child's position within the levels. If your child is recorded as having achieved a Level 4a in a subject, this means she is just short of a Level 5, whereas a Level 4c will have further to go. Roughly speaking, it is expected that it will take in the region of three years for a child to move up a level in her work. This can be frustrating, as parents often don't understand the amount of time it takes to progress up the levels and conclude that if their child is attaining the same level for two years, no progress has been made. Sub-levels show progress within a level, so parents don't think their children are not responding to or benefiting from their education.

All this is complicated by the fact that when it comes to work assessed by the teacher, the teacher will often – how shall I put this? – cheat. Teacher-assessed levels are often unreliable. A teacher will want to give parents the best possible idea of their child's progress under his tutelage, consequently grade inflation is all too common. Because the levelling is so absurdly complex, less experienced teachers will sometimes be caused to pick a number out of the air and apply it to your child's work. Be wary, therefore, of grades awarded by teachers with fresh faces, enthusiastic demeanours and shiny eyes. This is not to question their professionalism. The dynamism and idealism of newly qualified teachers can often be a real example to those a little longer in the tooth. In my experience, however, it takes a couple of years (at least) to get a really good grasp on levelling students' work correctly.

After they've been in the job for a good few years, teachers will reduce the complexity of the levels to their own simplified version for where a child is in terms of her written work. Here is mine:

Level 1 – can't write a sentence yet

Level 2 – can just about write a sentence

Level 3 – can write quite a few sentences, and uses the occasional comma, though usually in the wrong place

Level 4 – can use commas with a reasonable degree of accuracy

Level 5 – writes well; commas and a variety of punctuation are used accurately

Level 6 – writes very well; starts her sentences in a variety of ways, and gives them a variety of lengths; uses a full range of punctuation and connectives

Level 7 – writes better than you do, with style and fluency; knows where to put a colon and semi-colon

Loosely speaking – and provided your child doesn't take Years 10 and 11 off to smoke weed and mug old ladies – achieving the following NCAT Levels at the age of eleven will translate into these levels and GCSE grades at the ages of fourteen and sixteen respectively:

Attainment at eleven (Primary School Standard Assessment Tests)	Likely attainment at fourteen (Secondary School SATs)	Likely attainment at sixteen (GCSEs)
5 4 3 2* 1*	Exceptional Performance 7 6 5 4 3 2* 1*	A* A B C D E F G U

* Where a child falls below a Level 3 in her SATs exams, she is not awarded a grade.

The levels that teachers and students are chasing are those in bold. It is perceived as vital for a child to reach Level 4, specifically in English, by the age of eleven; a Level 5 in secondary school SATs and a C grade in GCSE are also significant benchmarks. The percentage of children in a year group achieving five A* to C passes is what the government's league tables are based on, as it is attainment of these grades that gives your child a pass towards A levels, and from there on to university.

So, if your child has achieved Level 5 in maths, science and English by the age of fourteen, she is on course for decent grades at GCSE, and you can breathe a sigh of relief. If she is still at Level 3 or 4 at this stage, it will take a whole lot of work and perhaps a new attitude to study for her to achieve C grade GCSE passes.

Accurate assessment does require years of professional experience, however, and it would be inadvisable to enter into an argument with a teacher about his grading, as he will know far more than you. Still, if you are seriously concerned about the grades your child is achieving in class, you should take the opportunity to speak to her teacher, who will be all too happy that you are taking such an interest, and will come up with a set of targets and a programme for improvement that will see her grades improve.

Formative Assessment

Constructive feedback about a child's work is called formative assessment. There is no mark involved, you don't have to have years of experience to fathom it out, and it is of vastly more educational worth than the summative variety.

The idea of formative assessment is that it gives children information on what they have done well, and what they need to do to improve. It's that simple. However, with the amount of pressure teachers are under from all kinds of pointless paperwork, it is one of the things that is easiest for us to let slip. You'll get crucified if you don't plan a lesson for your most difficult class, but you can get away with not marking books properly for weeks. When teachers have their lessons observed by a member of senior management or an OFSTED inspector, furious catching up is the order of the day. This is next door to useless for the kids, as the gradational process through which regular and rigorous marking causes children to acquire new knowledge is lost. It also tends to backfire really badly on the poor teacher. You can bet that the very moment the OFSTED inspector walks in the room, some loose-tongued student will shout out, 'Christ, sir, you've marked our books! He's marked our books, everybody! The first time in two years!' This can be poor reward for having gone without sleep for three days, catching up.

It is formative assessment that is of educational use to your child, and you can do a version of this at home. Your child might not relish your involvement in her education, but be strong here, for it is key to her success. Parental interest and involvement are a vital influence on high academic attainment, and the feedback you give your child about her work is as valuable as any teacher's. However, there is obviously a demarcation issue here. Actually marking your child's schoolbook is going to make her teacher either scared or angry, so it's best that the feedback you give is done verbally.

Constructive assessment requires a keen eye. You must be positive and encouraging about the work, but there's no point in a child labouring under the misapprehension that a mistake is anything other than that. Note down every spelling error, and every occasion when your child ignores the school rules for presentation of work.

There are teachers who think that putting swathes of red ink across a child's work makes that child feel she has got it all wrong, and leads to emotional collapse. There are also berks who refuse to mark in red, choosing green ink or pencil instead. A lot of hot air is wasted on this irrelevance in staffrooms across the country every day. But it isn't true that rigorous marking of children's efforts puts them off. What puts them off making an effort is when they have written a decent piece of work and nobody can be bothered to read it or remark upon it. There is no point whatsoever in a child going through life with her spelling mistakes uncorrected. If you write the word 'separate' with three 'e's in it and no one ever corrects it, you will continue under the misapprehension that 'seperate' is the correct spelling. If, on the other hand, it is continually pointed out to you that the word has two 'e's and two 'a's, it will sink in. So, a decent teacher will correct the spelling of every single word in at least the first paragraph. If, however, it turns out that every second word is misspelt, a good teacher will employ discretion. There's no point in correcting every spelling in that case, as the child has a serious learning disability and the teacher needs to be judicious as to how he approaches this.

As the teacher goes through your child's work he will notice things about it, good and bad. In the space at the bottom of the writing he will make some formative comments. The majority of these should be positive, but there should be room for two or three targets for improvement. These comments should be as voluminous as time permits. Kids judge how carefully a teacher has read their work on the basis of the amount of writing they have bothered to put at the bottom of it. A long comment – and by this I don't mean waffle – means that the child's work, and by implication the child herself, has been taken seriously; a short comment indicates to the child that the teacher doesn't care much about what she has written. Teachers who indulge in the 'tick everything and write "very good" at the bottom' approach to marking aren't taking this fantastic means of advancing their students' learning seriously enough.

There is no magic bullet in education. It's perspiration rather than inspiration, and good, effective, sustained marking is the single most important key to any child's academic improvement.

If you are reading your child's work and want to give her some verbal feedback on it, it helps if you have a pen and paper handy. As you read through, as soon as you notice something, jot it down. Don't save it up until you've read the whole thing, because then you will find that by the time you reach the end that brilliant thing you were going to tell your child which was in an instant going to transform her academic life has been forgotten. If the thing you've noticed is positive, then all the better: start your formative comment by saying, 'Fantastic, the use of commas here is brilliant,' or, 'I love the description of the bicycle seat's face as the bum sits on it.' If what you have seen is something your child could work on, give her a target and get her to record it in her school planner.

The kind of marking a serious professional will give your child might look something like this:

Fantastic. The description of the 'all-embracing globes of blubber descending on to the frowning seat' is exceptional descriptive writing because it uses imaginative adjectives. You have hit all the senses. Not many people manage to include the olfactory sense in their writing, and your paragraphing is exceptional.

<u>Targets – in your next piece of writing:</u>
1 Remember to put a comma before 'but'.
2 Try to vary the way in which you start sentences.
3 Try not to use the same word twice in a sentence.

The psychology behind this is quite simple. By using praise first, your child's teacher puts her in a relaxed and happy emotional state. When we are happy we are more open to being told that there are things we can do better. Double simple. Those targets should, as far as possible, be technical, focused on ways in which the writing can be improved. Teachers who concentrate solely on presentation either don't know what they are doing or simply can't be arsed.

The next part of the process is the teacher checking to make sure your child has hit the targets listed on her last piece. If she hasn't, the teacher should refer your child back to those targets. If your child has hit the targets, the teacher will note this fact, praising it.

Education is gradational. We build on what we already have, and it comes in the smallest steps, which can take the longest of times. It is built brick by tiny brick, but the diminutive size of these bricks should not in any way be congruent with the size of celebration of any achievement. When you can see from your child's work that she has scaled one of these steps by hitting one of the targets her teacher has given her, she has every reason to be proud of herself. Congratulate her, tell her that what she has done is fantastic, and bung her a small gift as a reward.

Assessment for learning

'Assessment for learning', as I understand it, revolves around the fundamental truth that unless you know what the gaps in a child's knowledge are, you don't have much chance of teaching her what she needs to know. My favourite line of the many thousand I have now written for the *Guardian* is this: 'Any fool can come up with a five-step lesson plan (formulated in the five steps before you get to the classroom door), but a teacher who knows exactly who her children are, and what it is they need to learn, is a teacher who is armed with fistfuls of gold and magic.' The concept of teachers being armed with fistfuls of gold and magic as they enter a class is one that really appeals to me. It is formative assessment that equips teachers with this, and it can equip interested parents with the same.

If you regularly read through your child's work, give her your thoughts on what she has done that is great or special, and include your views on where any weaknesses lie, and you are able to translate this always into positive feedback, you too will be armed with fistfuls of magic and gold. Sustained, positive interest in your child's work will not only affect her enthusiasm for doing it, and doing it well, it will affect the way in which she perceives work, and creativity itself. If you learn as a child that any positive effort you make brings congratulations from the most important people in your life – your parents – it'll stay with you. It will be encoded in your DNA that happiness is the by-product of positive action, and that will make happiness all the more readily attainable.

11
Revision and Exam Techniques

A couple of weeks after the half-term holiday in the summer of Year 11, you may find you have a sixteen-year-old at home who has too much time on his hands. They call this strange ritual, in which young people hang around the home kicking their heels and making the place look untidy, study leave. It can feel strange to parents to have a child they thought was in full-time education spending half the day in bed, particularly if you have sent your child to a fee-paying school. You might feel you have paid good money for nothing during this period. And you would be right.

Study leave exists so that the timetable can be cleared for exams. At least this is what you'll be led to believe. There may be other reasons. The last half-term of their life at a school can be a worrying time for Year 11 students. If the school does not have a sixth form, they will be leaving both the place and the people who have provided security and comfort for them over the space of five years. Facing the imminent dissolution of the certainty a school provides for them can lead young people into parlous emotional states, and those not skilled in managing their emotions can behave unpredictably. Basically, half of them go completely mental, and by the time the whole year group is escorted, en masse, off the site, many will have caused untold grief to their teachers, who though sad to see them go will also be breathing a hearty sigh of collective relief.

What sixteen-year-olds are supposed to be doing when they are on study leave is revising. Just as in the exam itself, the key to effective revision is sound time management – and when it comes to revision and exams, as in life itself, there's never quite as much time as you think.

SUCCESSFUL REVISION

Timetabling

Students should spend the morning of the first day of study leave constructing a detailed revision timetable. This should include time off during the days when they are revising and one whole day off at the weekend. Having devised the plan, it should be agreed with you, the parents, so that if your child is not at his desk slaving away, it is because he is in a timetabled period of relaxation to which you have consented.

So far as the amount of revision is concerned, your child should aim to cover a minimum of three different subjects every day, and these should be a balance of those he enjoys and those he doesn't. This way, he won't face the impenetrable barrier of a whole day being spent on something he finds as appealing as cold, salty porridge.

A decent revision timetable might look something like the chart below and overleaf:

Day	Morning	Afternoon	Evening
Sun	*Maths:* Exercises 1–9	*English (Lang):* Revise criteria of 'writing to persuade', then do mock exam. Mum to read.	*Science:* Re-read exercise book, highlighting salient points. Write list of topics I'm weak on.

Day	Morning	Afternoon	Evening
Mon	*French:* Write passage about holidays using irregular verbs, then rehearse this out loud as preparation for orals.	*Sociology:* Use ideology cards [see chapter 4] to go through the first page of Marx and Engels from different perspectives. Write these up and highlight key points, transferring on to summary cards.	*Geography:* Draw coloured diagrams of climate systems and water cycle to go up in bedroom.
Tue	*English (Lit):* Make tape of me reading the first and last chapters of *Mice and Men*. Listen to tonight before bed.	*History:* Mind map [see chapter 5] of all I know about the Second World War.	*Maths:* Exercises 10–18 Note: Listen to *Mice and Men* tape.
Wed	*English (Lang):* Re-read answer to mock exam on Sunday with Mum's comments. Write down targets for improvement and try another question. Mum to read.	*Science:* Take first weak topic and mind map. Test on key words.	*French:* Revise past perfect and perfect tense. Babble Gabble this with Dad [see chapter 3] and see if I can do Story in a Bag exercise [chapter 3 again] in French.
Thu	*Sociology:* Re-read textbook section on Bernstein's labelling theory, highlighting key concepts. Transfer this into labelled diagram of child (if poss).	*Geography:* Transfer information from geomorphology diagram into a poem. Write a song to remember key concepts. Teach it to little brother.	*English (Lit):* Draw all the main images in Simon Armitage poem, and all those in Carol Ann Duffy. Stick them on board and see if I can link them.

Day	Morning	Afternoon	Evening
Fri	*History:* Timeline of major events leading up to assassination of Franz Ferdinand.	*Afternoon off to go bowling*	*Science:* Go over photosynthesis again. Transfer the information on to cards.
Sat	*Day off*	*Day off*	*Day off*

This is just one week's revision. The normal period of study leave will be in the region of a month. With a decent structure – and assuming your child sticks to it – he can get a hell of a lot of effective revision done in that period.

Within the space of a day there are times when it is easier to study. Many people find they are more effective in the morning. In devising his revision schedule, your child should bear this in mind, putting the harder, more active pieces of revision at the time of day when he feels he studies most effectively.

Some subjects are worthy of more revision than others. Though a maths teacher would tell you otherwise, there's not much revision you can do for this subject. Maths is a set of processes at which you must be competent, not a collection of information you must remember. Provided your child has done some practice on performing mathematical tasks to keep his brain in top nick, there is not much point in reading maths textbooks.

It's important not to forget that your child must also keep body and soul together during this period. Sleep and food are vital, as is proper hydration. There is not much point in revising yourself half to death so that what enters the exam hall is a barely functioning cadaver who has skimped on food and sleep in order to cement pieces of information into a brain that no longer functions. On the morning before the exam make sure your condemned child eats a hearty breakfast and drinks lots of water (there is some evidence that eating a few bananas in the morning is particularly good for the brain). This will ensure his brain is working at its optimum level when it is most needed.

However, the most important thing about revision is to ensure that it is planned. If your child has struggled to keep to the plan and is in a panic, you must take control. A bit of late revision is better than none at all. It is vital that you remain calm: panic will put him in the kind of emotional state that will lead him to write his name on the top of the paper and nothing else. I've seen this happen many times, to even the brightest of students, and it is little short of tragic. Above all, just let him know he should do his best, and that if he has done this, it doesn't matter what the grade is. You will still love him no matter what the result.

Revision techniques

You may remember sitting in front of a book as a child, just before exam time, bored as hell, willing the information to go in, only for there to remain an invisible barrier between book and brain which left the information just staring back at you, refusing to jump the grand canyon betwixt the two. This is where the following activities come in. They are called DARTs (directed activities related to texts), and they form the bridge between book and brain.

Reading on its own is not the most effective way of learning. Very little of the information goes in, and you have nothing concrete to show for it later on from which you might revise or which might reactivate your memory of it. Doing something active with the information you are reading ensures you will have better recall of it, when required. It is also good practice for extracting information from a body of text to a specific brief.

You'll need access to a photocopier for some of these activities, or a bit too much time on your hands – which, as a parent, is a bit like suggesting a vagrant will need plenty of spare cash, a warm fire and the readily available breast of Catherine Deneuve on which to lay his head.

Taking notes

Taking notes is, quite obviously, the most easily understandable of the things to do while reading. It's not that easy to do well, however, as students are sometimes constrained by ideas of presentation. The path to successful note-taking is twofold: go mad, then organize.

Notes are thoughts. If you spend all your time ensuring that your first thought is transcribed in peachy keen order, you may miss the second thought, which might be infinitely better. There is no point coming up with the most brilliant and original idea in the universe and saying to yourself, 'I'll jot that down when I've finished treble underlining the phrase "racism is naughty" in highlighter and red pen.' Thoughts flash across our minds momentarily, and if you don't catch that fantastic idea in the butterfly net that is your note-taking the moment it crosses your eyeline, it will flutter away. So, make sure your children don't give a toss about presentation when they are taking notes initially. Focusing overmuch on presentation is a form of unconscious self-censorship: it stops good stuff getting on to the page.

However, after a serious session of communing with some weighty text and jotting down whatever came into his head, your child will find that what he is left with is a page full of unintelligible spider footprints, which will make little sense to even the most experienced graphologist. He should take a break for a few minutes, then organize those brilliant ideas into something he'll understand when he returns to them. The 'tables' or 'segmenting' activities coming up are useful ways of organizing the notes. A mind map is useful too (see chapter 5). The point is that reprocessing the information into a different format, using it in a subtly different way, sorting through it, making decisions and categorizing, will cause the information to lodge in your child's brain.

Underlining

Something like this appears to speak for itself, but underlining the main features of an argument or picking out the most important facts from a page of dense prose is very useful. Senior examiners recommend that students underline the key facets of every exam question to ensure that they actually answer the one in front of them, rather than the one they wanted. Again, it's best if you have access to a photocopier here, as teachers are prone to look askance at children who return to school with their books covered with scribble, particularly if you have already torn out a page to do a sequencing activity. The purpose of this activity is to encourage kids to read a text and search for particular information, which they will then underline or circle.

Try this at home

Give your child a photocopied page from one of his school books, along with a brief as to what he should underline: for instance, it might help with his English homework to underline all the adjectives in a passage of text; for geography homework you might ask him to underline all the elements that might cause coastal erosion; for a science activity, you might ask that he underlines any mention of the key words he has been studying that week.

In addition to helping with comprehension, this method teaches children how to skim-read, which is a skill they'll need when they get to the last five minutes of an exam having answered only the first two questions.

Colour coding

This is a great technique for visual learners. Highlighter pens can be used when studying a text and attempting to extract, flag up or even, erm, highlight information under different headings. Use different colours to show where different themes are located. For English work, your child might use a pink, for instance, to highlight an author's use of irony, a blue for a specific repeated image, and a yellow for use of alliteration.

This activity comes into its own at revision time. It's always useful to purchase a see-through pack containing assorted highlighters a couple of months before exams begin. Rather than have your child staring blindly at a page and calling it revision, liberal use of varied highlighters makes it an active task, and gives him a sense that he is not just bashing his head against a brick wall.

A variant on this makes use of modern technology. If a child is retyping his notes as a revision exercise, he can do so ensuring that the most vital pieces of information are in bigger fonts or different colours. This will make all the difference when he is using the notes for cramming before the exams.

Tables

Boys love tables. Not the kind you'd need to know something about joinery to build. I mean the kind of table you do work in, not on; the type you'd find as an option on a word processor. Oh sod it. You've met them before in this book, but just to make sure there's no confusion, here's what one looks like:

Characteristics of a wooden table	Characteristics of a paper table
It's wooden (of course)	You can't put much on it
It's got four legs	It hasn't got any legs
It sometimes has drawers	It rarely has drawers
It's made by a carpenter	It's made by a schoolchild or a teacher writing a book

The trouble with boys' passion for 'doing a table' is that their professed joy for this exercise may actually be a skilled and surreptitious work-avoidance tactic. Drawing the table itself can take anything up to an hour, and woe betide the teacher who tells them that they haven't done any work at all. They'll simply point at the empty boxes they have drawn on their page and ask indignantly, 'What's that then, sir? An apparition?' So, if your child is using tables to help him revise, make sure he doesn't spend his whole time just drawing the table. It doesn't matter what it looks like, it matters what's in it.

Taking information from a text and putting it into tabular form is another way of ensuring that students read the text closely. They must scour it in order to locate the stuff to go in the table. The tables might have several columns, and can be on any topic. For instance, this is what a table on Shakespeare's mentions of root vegetables in *Othello* would look like:

Turnip	Beetroot	Carrot	Parsnip	Potato
Iago to Roderigo: 'Th'art as tasty as a turnip, as rambunctious as a radish.'	Iago to Roderigo: 'Taketh thy visage away, thou beetroot-faced loon.'	Iago to Othello: 'It is said abroad that Cassio possesses a fine and noble carrot.'	Iago to Othello: 'Rumour has it that his parsnip is also right royal.'	Emilia to Desdemona: 'For men, we are but potatoes and they are fond of lots of different varieties of crisps.'

With all of these exercises, the cognitive part of searching for the information, which embeds knowledge far more effectively than reading alone, is combined with producing a piece of work that will be a useful reference for revision. This table is a case in point. I have remembered these (honestly not fictional – raises eyebrow) vegetable references off the top of my head a full twenty-four years after having done this table some time in the lower sixth.

Segmenting

Segmenting is what one would do with larger, more complex pieces of information, which your child might need to group together. You may know this as 'taking notes under headings'. Much like city academies, and specialist schools, segmenting a text is firmly in the territory of 'same old thing in brand-new clothes'. Its advantage over putting notes in table form is that there is more room. It is not constrained by the spatial strictures of the table, and as such, provided you have left enough room between headings, there's no limit to the amount or complexity of information you can record.

Let's take a critical analysis of 'The Heartbreaking Tale of Terrence and Garreth' as a start. The story, I'll remind you, goes like this: 'Once upon a time there were two Welsh mice called Terrence and Garreth. They decided that they would live together and accordingly built a cosy and charming home. The roof fell in and they died.' An analysis of it might be segmented under the following headings: 'Use of Generic Convention', 'Homoerotic Undertones' and 'The Welsh Angle'. You would first write the headings on separate pages, then make notes under the headings shown overleaf:

Use of Generic Convention

☞ The tightly defined use of an identifiable beginning, middle and end mark this out as a classic chronological narrative.

☞ Temporally, it is orthodox.

☞ Note also that it is described as a 'home', not just a house. This implies that the mice have populated it with their possessions and have spent time settling before the roof fell in on them.

☞ Note the use of the standard fairy-tale phrase 'Once upon a time' at the start. This sets up expectations as to audience and form.

Homoerotic Undertones

☞ There is an underlying question surrounding the relationship of the two mice. I suspect that the conclusion that they are gay lovers is too simple.

☞ It is entirely reasonable to conclude that Terrence and Garreth are simply flat-mates. (Perhaps the fact that they die, splatted, beneath a collapsed roof is a deliberate and wilful pun on this.)

☞ There is a possibility that the author is using our generic expectations, set up by the fairy-tale beginning, as a satire on the mice's sexuality. A fairy tale would generally feature at least one evil queen. Why not two innocent ones?

☞ The names Terrence and Garreth have symmetrical properties, leading one to conclude that they are, in fact, mirror images of each other; that they fit together, so to speak. (Terrence Fitzgarreth and Garreth Fitzterrence.)

The Welsh Angle

☞ There'll be a welcome in the hillsides at such a 'cosy' and 'comfortable' home.

☞ The author states emphatically and nakedly that the mice are 'Welsh', and this is further confirmed by their names. 'Terrence' and 'Garreth', with the repeated 'r' in the middle of the names, are peculiarly Welsh spellings.

Should 'The Heartbreaking Tale of Terrence and Garreth' ever become a set GCSE text – and I am hopeful – the above would hit an A* grade right on the nose. The criteria for getting an A* in English state the vital importance of 'originality of analysis and interpretation'. By leaving himself a large space for notes, which he may not always fill, your child allows himself the possibility of going to the further reaches of analysis, where, when combined with organization and academic discipline, the highest levels of achievement are possible.

SUCCESSFUL EXAMS

More so than is the case with revision, the exams themselves require serious time management skills. There are some techniques that *must* be used in exams if your child wants to give as good an account of himself as possible, and get the grade he deserves.

Time management

This is the most crucial area, where the brightest of students can go to pieces and completely sabotage years of hard work by ignoring one relatively simple instruction. Managing his time in the exam hall is the thing your child absolutely must do well if he is not to balls it all up and come home sobbing. You may adopt as stern a voice as you wish while imparting this piece of information.

Exams are brutal. There is no room for manoeuvre in any of them. They are, in fact, more a test of your child's ability to manage his time than of what he knows.

A hypothetical situation, to illustrate. There are three questions worth a combined total of a hundred marks in an exam that lasts one hour. The first question is worth twenty marks, the second is worth thirty, and the last worth fifty. If your child spends half an hour on the first question, he has completely, totally and utterly screwed up his chances of doing well in the exam. Once you have made such an error, there is no room whatsoever during an exam to retrieve the situation. By spending half the time on a fifth of the marks, he will have left himself the other half of the time to obtain the remaining four fifths. It can't be done.

Exams as a form of assessment have the potential to lead to complete heartbreak if this timekeeping rule is not observed. I have witnessed the most fantastic students ruin two years of creative hard work by failing to commune with the time constraints involved (including, to my sadness and horror, the brilliant Funmi, who took on John Humphrys so fearlessly).

The *very first thing* your child should do in any written exam is work out how the marks available translate into portions of time. Exactly. In the example above, he should have spent twelve minutes on question one, eighteen minutes on question two and a full half-hour on question three. Once he has these timings, *he must stick to them*. There is no point whatsoever in gaining full marks for a question that is worth almost nothing while answering a more heavily weighted question in a token manner.

A further word of warning. The shadowy spinsters who sit hunched in drafty attics setting these inhuman tortures are nothing if not cunning. They are aware that children are liable to spend a disproportionate amount of time on the first question, so they give these scanty marks. There is a significant argument in favour of your child, once he has worked out the amount of time he has for each answer, tackling the one with the most marks first. This will often be the last question in any written exam. It takes a bit of guts, but it ensures he does not risk the possibility of leaving little time for the most important question on the paper.

This may be the most serious piece of advice contained in this book. Treat it as such.

The other secret to exam success

In the last lesson before their GCSE exams, after lecturing my students on how vital time management is when sitting an exam, I present every one of them with an envelope. It is labelled 'The Secret to Exam Success' and it contains a single piece of paper. On that piece of paper are the words 'Answer . . . the . . . bloody . . . question'.

Exams are tricksy, and there is a temptation for students to answer the question they have revised for, rather than the one in front of them. To counter this possibility examiners advise students to underline the key words in the question, to help them be sure that they know what the examiner is asking them. For example, here is a writing task from a past SATs paper: 'Write an article for a travel magazine, describing a place that is beautiful but mysterious.' Underlining the key words *article*, *travel magazine*, *beautiful* and *mysterious* will give your child a clearer idea of the format required, the audience he is writing for and what he must include in his answer. After going through this process he will have identified exactly what the examiner wants of him and can move on to planning his response.

Planning

Most teachers will advise that students plan their responses before launching into the writing, and this, of course, is a good idea. There is an issue, though. Teachers are so keen on planning that they tend to overstate its importance, to the extent that you sometimes find children in an exam room spending so long on it there is no time for the actual writing.

The amount of planning your child does for a question should take account of the marks available. Planning the response should take about a quarter of all the time allocated for that question. So, in a one-hour exam with three questions and a hundred marks, your child should calculate on:

Question 3 (50 marks) – 8 minutes' planning, 22 minutes' writing
Question 2 (30 marks) – 5 minutes' planning, 13 minutes' writing
Question 1 (20 marks) – 3 minutes' planning, 9 minutes' writing

Your child could start his plan in the form of a brainstorm before organizing it into logical paragraphs.

The plan for the SATs question asking for an article for a travel magazine might look like this:

1   Setting: where it is in Europe, description of beach, exotic insects and restaurants, sand-spit peninsula
2   Beautiful: lunar landscape, cotton castles, azure sea, boats
3   Mysterious: skydiving, deserted village, Ephesus, statues of Artemis and only remaining wonder of the ancient world
4   Conclusion: why a tourist would like to go there; cost implications and flight times

A plan is as brief as this, but it gives your child a structure he can refer to during the process of writing the essay. He is unlikely to go off on some unrewarding tangent that doesn't answer the question. He will, instead, answer the question in a concise and organized manner.

Checking

If your child finishes the exam before the time allotted is up, he shouldn't just sit back in his chair, thinking, 'Thank God that's over. Look at what Kylie's wearing!' All time in an exam hall is precious. Advise him to use the time to read over every word, checking his answers and making corrections as he goes.

Relaxation

When the senior invigilator requests that students turn over their papers and start the exam, the usual response is for every student in the room to do this at the speed an Olympic sprinter might leave the blocks. This is counter-productive. They launch into such a fevered rush of activity that it impairs their ability to think clearly. I advise students to count to ten in their heads before turning over their papers. That way they start the exam calmly, and are able to think straight as they read the paper and underline the key words.

Attitude to exams

Every year, in the last lesson before my students go on study leave, I'll lay out a ruler and an exam paper on every desk. Each student is then asked to pick up the exam paper with their right hand and to dangle it between two fingers, while grasping the ruler in their left fist. They are then to bring the ruler to the backside of the exam paper and, at teacher's request, to 'spank its arse'. They enjoy doing this enough for it to be worth the time on my knees picking up pieces of shredded exam papers which lie like ticker tape at an Argentinian football match in every corner of the classroom.

The point here is that positive attitude is everything in the exam room. They are entering a gladiatorial environment in which a strong heart is every bit as important as any knowledge they have acquired. It may be that the questions the examiner has set them are all on the one thing they failed to revise for. It may be that the paper is just too bloody difficult for them. If this is the case, then the exam becomes a test of moral strength. The child who folds in the exam room potentially sabotages his chances in life. It is that important. The child who rolls up his sleeves, mouths, 'Shit, this is difficult,' and gets on with it is likely to do well.

During the period leading up to exams, ask your child to mouth the mantra 'Whatever happens in there I am not going to be put off doing my best – and my best is good enough'. Get him to repeat it to himself just before he enters the exam room, and before he turns over the paper, and then tell him to perform whatever version of 'spank its arse' you find most palatable.

There's an old parable in which a wise man is sitting at a crossroads on the outskirts of a town. He is approached by a man who says to him, 'I'm moving to this town soon. Could you tell me, is it a nice place to live?'

The old man rubs his beard and replies, 'What's it like where you live now?'

'It's wonderful. The neighbours are great and the streets are full of sunshine.'

'That's what it's like here,' says the grizzled wise one.

After a few hours have passed a second man approaches.

'I'm moving to this town soon,' he says. 'Could you tell me, is it a nice place to live?'

The old man starts rubbing his chin again and comes back with the same question: 'What's it like where you live now?'

'It's terrible,' the second man replies. 'The neighbours are awful and it's always raining.'

'That's what it's like here,' says the wise one.

Attitude is everything. This applies not only to exams, but to the whole of your child's school life. If he can enter the school gates with the knowledge that education is the most fantastic of all the adventures he will have in his life, then you, his parent, will have done him proud.

It only remains for me to say, good luck.

Acknowledgements

Heidi Stephenson, Linda Powell, Jonathan Gillard (who nominated me for an award), Ann Palmer (an extremely supportive head teacher), Jo Shuter and Jeffrey Leader (who gave me the award), and John Sutton (who assessed me for another one). Special thanks go to Will Woodward (who claims that he 'made me', and is probably right) and to Ted and Judith Wragg.

Claire Phipps, who commissioned me to write an article, which caused the remarkable and now much-loved Geraldine Cooke to get in touch, who, in turn, put me into the warm, guiding hands of Marianne Velmans, Sarah Westcott and Daniel Balado.

Any child who has had the bad luck to have to spend day after day in a classroom in Canning Town with a dangerous lunatic at the front, particularly my form groups, 7D featuring the fantastic four and 10S. All the kids in *The Unteachables*, especially Dale, Grace, Finbar, Shane and Zaak.

And mainly to Jennifer Eirlys Owens, Bazzy, Len, Lou, Ken and Olive Beadle.

Bibliography

Brindley, Susan (ed.), *Teaching English* (Open University, 1994)

Buzan, Tony, *How to Mindmap: The Ultimate Thinking Tool that Will Change Your Life* (Thorsons, 2002)

Caviglioli, Oliver, Harris, Ian and Tindall, Bill, *Thinking Skills and Eye Q: Visual Tools for Raising Intelligence* (Network Educational Press, 2002)

De Bono, Edward, *Six Thinking Hats* (Penguin, 1985)

Gardner, Howard, *Frames of Mind: Theory of Multiple Intelligence* (Fontana Press, 1993)

Gilbert, Ian, *Essential Motivation in the Classroom* (RoutledgeFalmer, 2002)

Gilbert, Ian (ed.), *The Big Book of Independent Thinking* (Crown House, 2006)

Goleman, Daniel, *Emotional Intelligence* (Bantam Books, 1995)

Levine, David A., *Teaching Empathy: A Blueprint for Caring, Compassion and Community* (Solution Tree, 2005)

Morris, Desmond, *The Human Animal* (BBC Books, 1994)

Truss, Lynne, *Eats, Shoots and Leaves* (Profile, 2003)

Wilson, Gary, *Breaking the Barriers to Boys' Achievement* (Networkcontinuum, 2006)

Index

CHILD OF OUR TIME: EARLY LEARNING
By Dr Tessa Livingstone

What makes children intelligent, resourceful, creative and flexible? Their minds are the powerhouse for everything they think and do and are shaped crucially by the knowledge they gain when they are very young.

At the very beginning, newborn babies are ready and eager to learn, but by the time children start school, five years later, many will have lost their all-embracing excitement for learning. So what can you do to hone your children's skills? How can you improve their motivation, concentration and intelligence?

Child of Our Time: Early Learning will help you discover:

- How your learning styles can help your child
- How to give your child a strong, flexible memory
- How to help your child with words, maths or art through the early school years
- What to do so your child gains a love of learning that will last a lifetime

Using cutting-edge research in neurology, psychology, genetics and sociology, together with the personal experiences of the families featured on BBC1's *CHILD OF OUR TIME* series, Dr Tessa Livingstone, herself a mother of two, guides parents through the crucial period in a young child's life that will shape their intelligence and their future.

9780593059272

WHAT REALLY WORKS FOR KIDS
The Insider's Guide to Natural Health for Mums and Dads
By Susan Clark

What is the greatest gift you can give your child? Vibrant good health, of course. But in a world where children as young as ten are being diagnosed with early signs of heart disease, where up to a third of youngsters at an infants' school may be taking Ritalin, a drug that has been banned in Sweden, and where a computer, not a dog is a child's best friend, how do you get it right?

In *What Really Works for Kids*, Susan Clark, award-winning *Sunday Times* journalist and one of Britain's leading natural health writers, draws upon years of experience and the very latest scientific research to offer every parent the opportunity to make sound, confident decisions that will benefit their children's health now and in the future.

Here, as she highlights the the health hazards that plagaue so many youngsters today and unravels the complex and often contradictory information that appears in the media, Susan offers invaluable advice and information on:

- the use of vitamins, herbs and homeopathic treatments that can really make a difference to a child's health

- hands-on therapies, such as infant massage and hand reflexology

- the fascinating key stages of development, from newborn to young adulthood

- how to treat over fify everyday childhood complaints

- a range of relaxing and quick-fix treats to help busy mums and dads cope with those particularly stressful days

Practical and comprehensive, *What Really Works for Kids* is the ultimate alternative health guide for parents everywhere – and one of the most valuable books they will ever own.

9780593049198

A CHILD AGAINST ALL ODDS
By Robert Winston

In a single act of coitus, the famously fecund rabbit has a 9 per cent chance of producing up to twelve offspring. By comparison humans are infertile animals. The average chance of conception in the UK is about 18 per cent per month and more than one in ten couples experience difficulty in conceiving.

Unprecedented demand for infertility treatments has pushed scientific innovation dangerously close to the boundaries of what is ethical. We are only years away from being able to alter human genetics to eradicate disease and to create so-called designer babies – a frightening prospect to many. In vitro fertilization, it seems, has become big business. But at what cost?

Robert Winston has spent his professional life at the forefront of this most fascinating and emotive area of science and has been responsible for many of the recent advances in treating human infertility. *A Child Against All Odds* is his definitive account of modern reproductive technology and the ethical problems that it raises. Hard-hitting, sometimes humorous, always honest, *A Child Against All Odds* is highly engaging for the general reader and essential reading for anyone facing infertility and IVF treatments.

'Erudite and accessible, powerful and humane'
Independent on Sunday

'[Winston] traces the awesome history of reproductive medicine from myth to the latest breakthroughs in stem-cell research and DNA manipulation . . . His account is magisterial'
Sunday Telegraph

9780553817447

LET'S TALK SEX
Everything you need to know about sex – without going behind the bike sheds!
By Davina McCall and Anita Naik

So, you've survived the sleepless nights, the midnight feeds and the terrible twos, but now the first days of school are approaching and it's time to think about preparing your children for the big, bad world. But how do you look after their emotional health? How can you build their self-esteem? And how do you start preparing them for adult life so that when they are faced with new, exciting or even intimidating grown-up situations they have the confidence to make strong, informed decisions?

Here, in their companion to Channel 4's *Let's Talk Sex*, Davina McCall and Anita Naik set out to answer all these questions and more. Packed full of information on everything from puberty and self-esteem to contraception and pregnancy, this practical and no-nonsense guide to sex, emotional health and relationships will help you to talk comfortably to your children, whatever their age. There is a comprehensive sex test that will show you just how much you know about the birds and the bees and Q&A sections to help you answer those really difficult questions should you get stuck. There are also a number of 'parent-free zones' so your children can read the facts of life for themselves.

As tempting as it is to bury your head in the sand and hope they will learn everything they need from their teachers and their friends, research shows that children who can talk to their parents are much more likely to delay sex until they're ready and to practise safe sex when they do take the plunge. So be brave, take a deep breath, sit your children down and get talking. You never know, they may even thank you for it!

9781905026180

THE LAST GENERATION
How Nature will take her revenge for Climate Change
By Fred Pearce

'Apocalyptic in its vision, but never scare-mongering, *The Last Generation* superbly explains and dramatizes both the causes and the consequences of climate change. One reads it both gripped and deeply alarmed'
ROBERT MACFARLANE

Since the last ice age, almost 13,000 years ago, humans have prospered in a stable, predictable climate. But our generation is the last to be so blessed. In *The Last Generation* Fred Pearce lays bare the terrifying prognosis for our planet now being sketched out in learned scientific journals. We are at a tipping point. Climate change from now on will not be gradual, maintains Pearce – nature doesn't do gradual change. In the past, Europe's climate has switched from Arctic to tropical in three to five years. It can happen again. So forget what environmentalists have told you about nature being fragile, a helpless victim of human excess. The truth is the opposite. She is a wild and resourceful beast given to fits of rage. And now that we are provoking her beyond endurance, she is starting to seek her revenge.

'We are now at war with Gaia and have no chance whatever of winning. Fred Pearce's scholarly and thoughtful book analyzes the battlefield and will guide us in a sensible retreat to the place where we can negotiate a peace'
JAMES LOVELOCK

'Fred Pearce has sounded the final warning . . . It is as if we are all on a plane with the auto-pilot set to crash'
THE RT HON JOHN GUMMER MP

Read this book. Your children's future depends on it.

9781903919873

A CHILD IS BORN
By Lennart Nilsson and Lars Hamberger

When it was first published nearly forty years ago, Lennart Nilsson's *A Child is Born* broke astonishing new ground, offering an unprecedented glimpse of life inside the womb. Now this completely new fourth edition brings revolutionary photographic technology and artistry to a landmark work. Packed with breathtaking, never-before-seen photographs and entirely new text, this awesome journey from fertilization to birth is a timeless masterpiece – completely revised for a new generation.

Long considered the world's leading medical and scientific photographer, Lennart Nilsson uses a new high-definition ultrasound technique, scanning electron and light microscopes, and advanced fibre optics to make an unparalleled record of the unseen world within our bodies. Here, in a series of stunning close-up images, the miracle of human reproduction unfolds: The egg travelling down the Fallopian tube; the sperm racing to meet it; the moment of fertilization; the very first cell division; the tiny embryo attaching to the uterine wall; the growth of eyes, ears, fingers, and toes; and finally the moment of delivery itself – are revealed with brilliant artistry, in full colour. These historic photos – which include over 350 that are new to this edition – give an astonishing glimpse of the first moments of life. And the updated text by longtime collaborator Lars Hamberger features authoritative advice for new parents, plus fascinating information on recent advances in fertility treatments, state-of-the-art testing, genetics, environmental factors, and pregnancy health.

A treasured reference for the entire family, this brand-new edition of the perennial classic is at once a compelling reading experience and a visual adventure – the finest introduction to the universal miracle of birth.

9780385606714